The Scope and Authority of the Bible

BOOKS BY JAMES BARR
Published by The Westminster Press

The Scope and Authority of the Bible
Fundamentalism

The Scope
and Authority
of the Bible

BY
JAMES BARR

THE WESTMINSTER PRESS
PHILADELPHIA

© James Barr 1980

First published in 1980 by SCM Press Ltd, London,
under the title *Explorations in Theology 7*

Published by The Westminster Press℞
Philadelphia, Pennsylvania

PRINTED IN THE UNITED STATES OF AMERICA
9 8 7 6 5 4 3 2 1

Library of Congress Cataloging in Publication Data

Barr, James.
The scope and authority of the Bible.

Bibliography: p.
Includes index.
1. Bible — Criticism, interpretation, etc. — Addresses,
essays, lectures. I. Title.
BS540.B323   1981   220.6   80-21394
ISBN 0-664-24361-4

Contents

Introduction

The seven essays published in this volume are united by a common interest in the nature, authority and use of the Bible; they represent the recent thinking of the author and develop further some of the lines of thought pursued in his earlier writings (see Bibliography), taking subsequent discussion into account. Some of the essays were originally lectures expressly designed for a specific occasion in a particular institution; but it seemed best not to remove by alterations the particularity of their origin, and they have been left substantially as they were. The present introduction furnishes any necessary explanation of the background, purpose and setting.

The first essay was originally the Third Nuveen Lecture, delivered in the Divinity School of the University of Chicago on 16 April 1975. It was published in *The Journal of Religion*, Vol. 56, No. 1, 1976, pp. 1–17, and is here reprinted from that journal by permission of the University of Chicago Press (© 1976 by The University of Chicago. All rights reserved). The essay is an attempt to state, in the short compass of a single lecture, a fresh synthetic view of the familiar problem of biblical narrative and its relation to history on the one hand, to theological substance on the other. The question has engaged the writer throughout many stages of his work, and the climate of opinion about it has been altering rapidly. The essay expresses the conviction that the great narrative complex of the Bible is indeed a powerful indicator of the character of biblical faith, but that that narrative substance is better designated as 'story' than as 'history'. On the other hand, it is quite right that history in a certain sense is basic to biblical faith: but the history which thus functions is not identical with the story told by the biblical texts.

The second essay was my Inaugural Lecture as Oriel Professor of the Interpretation of Holy Scripture in Oxford University; it was delivered on 26 May 1977. The relation between biblical study and theology has been an uneasy one in our time. Within theological curricula there is often some question concerning the balance of time, effort and influence that should be devoted to each. Moreover, biblical studies are no longer exclusively tied to a setting in theological faculties, but may be undertaken as part of a general humanistic, linguistic or historical education. Religious sentiment may suggest that, since the Bible is a document of faith, the interpretation of it can be carried out only in a context of faith. On the other hand, paradoxically, it may be argued that existing traditions and fashions of doctrine can easily distort or obscure the true meaning of the Bible, and that the Bible can do its best service for faith only when the study of it is loosed from doctrinal constraints. Perhaps, as this essay suggests, these two views, which seem so opposed, may be combined in a wholesome and salutary way.

The third essay concerns the historical reading of scripture and its relation to theological interpretation. In spite of the centrality of historical study for our understanding of the meaning of scripture, and in spite of the impressive gains in understanding that have been made since the rise of it, there remains much uncertainty about the way in which it relates to theology itself. Even if the historical reading of scripture has been, and is, helpful to theology, does it remain in itself essentially a *secular* approach and one lacking in justification from within theology itself? Or, on the other hand, are there good theological reasons why historical reading – which by its nature must also be *critical* reading – is desirable and indeed necessary if the Bible is to be free to carry out its theological functions? The paper was first read at the Sixth International Congress on Biblical Studies, Oxford, 3–7 April 1978, and was also delivered as the Armstrong Lecture in Victoria University, Toronto, on 21 March 1979.

The essay entitled 'Has the Bible any authority?' is of rather more popular character and attempts to press into a short space the essentials of a viable answer to that question. The question itself was proposed to the author by the organizers of a series of open lectures on matters of revelation and authority in Cambridge in April, 1979. The presentation is intended to be of a level suitable for an audience that is intelligent and generally informed but not technically trained in theology.

All discussions of biblical authority lead one in due course to consider the phenomenon of fundamentalism, and my book *Fundamentalism* was published in 1977. Since then I have been involved in a great deal of discussion and have read further papers in a variety of centres in several countries. In addition, many personal letters, visits and interviews have given me a vivid further perception of the deep perplexity and often suffering experienced by people who either themselves or through their dear ones are caught up in the influence of fundamentalism. The essay offers a concise statement of major aspects of the subject, in so far as it can be handled within a single piece of limited length; and it includes some afterthoughts following my book and the subsequent discussions. Among the many lectures I have given on the subject I have particularly enjoyed those where the audience has been of more or less fundamentalist background or at least sympathetic with such background, as in the traditional 'Bible Belt' of the United States. Within such groups I have always been courteously received and listened to with respect. I have never found that the rather hard-hitting character of my criticisms in writing have formed an obstacle to communication: on the contrary, I think that it has favoured communication, and fundamentalists (rightly) do not particularly want to cover up the deep chasm of disagreement with false politeness or cheap praise. The sad thing is that, because of the peculiar character of fundamentalism, it is unlikely that any more than a tiny minority of fundamentalists will ever be able to hear a contrary voice at all, since the nature of the movement and its organizations is to prevent them from doing so.

The particular form of the paper here published is that read at the meeting of the South African Old Testament Society (Ou-Testamentiese Werkgemeenskap in Suider-Afrika) in Pretoria, August 1979, and it will be published also in the journal of that society, *OTWSA*. I would like here to express gratitude to that society for the honour it did to both myself and my wife in electing us as Honorary Members at that meeting.

The sixth essay, on 'The Bible as a political document', was originally a Ludwig Mond Lecture delivered in the University of Manchester on 14 February 1978. (A modified form of it was read also in the University of North Carolina at a Symposium on 'Interpretations of Religion and Culture' in March 1980.) In keeping with the wide social and scientific range of this distinguished series of lectures, the intention was to consider the broad cultural and social effects which the Bible has exercised, rather than to suggest ways in which political interpretations of the Bible for today should be produced. Nevertheless the perception of the ways in which the Bible has affected our political awareness in the past is of much importance for any understanding of the potential of its future application. This essay was originally published in the *Bulletin* of the John Rylands University Library, Manchester, Volume 62, Spring 1980.

The seventh essay was one of two keynote addresses in a special conference held in the University of Chicago Divinity School in October 1979. This conference on the Bible commemorated the coming to Chicago in 1879 of William Rainey Harper, then as professor in a Baptist seminary, but later to be instrumental in the founding of the University of Chicago and to become its first President. Harper was a major educationalist and did much for the study of the Old Testament, of Hebrew and of other Semitic languages. The conference also celebrated the opening of the Institute of Advanced Studies in Religion in the University of Chicago. There were two major keynote addresses in the conference. The first, delivered by Professor Gerhard Ebeling, took as subject 'The Bible as a document of the University'. The second, reprinted here, was on 'The Bible as a document of believing communities', and in this reference is made to its place in Judaism as well as its place in Christianity. This context explains the references in the essay to Harper and to Professor Ebeling's parallel presentation. Both papers together, along with another by Professor Paul Ricoeur and a Foreword by Martin E. Marty, will be published in a volume entitled: *The Bible as a Document of the University. Three Essays*, with a Foreword by Martin E. Marty, edited by Hans Dieter Betz (Missoula, Montana: Scholars Press, 1980). For me the invitation of the University of Chicago formed an opportunity, gladly received, to restate some basic outlines of ideas about the authority and function of the Bible, in the context of the dialectic between academic study and study within the community of faith.

I acknowledge with thanks the permission of the Editors of the *Journal of Religion* and the University of Chicago Press to republish the first essay, that of the Oxford University Press to republish the second, that of the South African journal *OTWSA* and its editors, Professors J. Loader and W. C. van Wyk, to republish the fifth, that of the *Bulletin* of the John Rylands University Library and its editor, Dr F. Taylor, F.S.A., to republish the sixth, and that of Professor H. D. Betz and the University of Chicago to republish the seventh.

Since readers may be interested in tracing other writings of the author, a bibliography of his main written works up to the end of 1979 is included.

Christ Church, Oxford J.B.

Abbreviations

BJRL	*Bulletin of the John Rylands Library*, Manchester
BZAW	Beihefte zur *Zeitschrift für die alttestamentliche Wissenschaft*, Berlin
ET	English translation
ExpT	*Expository Times*, Edinburgh
IDB Suppl	*Interpreter's Dictionary of the Bible*, Supplementary Volume, Abingdon Press 1976
JR	*Journal of Religion*, Chicago
JSS	*Journal of Semitic Studies*, Manchester
JTS	*Journal of Theological Studies*, Oxford
OS	*Oudtestamentische Studiën*, Leiden
PSB	*Princeton Seminary Bulletin*, Princeton, NJ
RTP	*Revue de Théologie et de Philosophie*, Lausanne
SEÅ	*Svensk exegetisk årsbok*, Lund
SBT	Studies in Biblical Theology, London and Naperville, Ill.
SJT	*Scottish Journal of Theology*, Edinburgh
ThStZ	Theologische Studien, Zürich
VT	*Vetus Testamentum*, Leiden
VTS	*Vetus Testamentum Supplements*, Leiden

Quotations from the Bible are normally from the Revised Standard Version.

1

Story and History in Biblical Theology[1]

There is no subject that has undergone greater convulsions in the last twenty-five years or that has suffered greater changes in its status and esteem than biblical theology. The years immediately following the Second World War saw it rising into pre-eminence and taking over much of the leadership in biblical studies, at least in such biblical studies as were theologically motivated or interested. Its high point was in the decade from 1950 to 1960. By that time people were claiming that biblical theology was the essential key to the theological problems of the churches and that it alone could heal the divisions between the church traditions, divisions that had been caused by the differing non-biblical elements which each tradition had accepted. From this period we remember the enormous influence gained by such typical works as O. Cullmann's *Christ and Time* or the late George Ernest Wright's *God Who Acts*[2] – this last work, I think, written here in Chicago. But the time during which biblical theology held the centre of the stage was destined to be short. Brevard Childs is exactly right when he writes:

> The Biblical Theology Movement underwent a period of slow dissolution beginning in the late fifties. The breakdown resulted from pressure from inside and outside the movement that brought it to a virtual end as a major force in American theology in the early sixties.[3]

The sudden decline of biblical theology has left, however, something of a sense of bewilderment. On the one hand, why did things go wrong? On the other hand, what is now to be done? Can one just exist without a biblical theology, or does one have to look for some other and quite different formula by which a future biblical theology will have to be carried out?[4]

Now I am not going to spend a lot of time on an inquest into the decline or decease of the older biblical theology, but I will mention a few aspects that are important for our subject today. First of all, as we see it today, the biblical theology of the period 1945–60 was far too much dominated by its reaction against the liberal theology and against the way in which biblical scholarship had behaved in the era of liberal theology. Many of the things that biblical theology maintained had an adequate *relative* justification when seen against the older liberal position (and equally against the older conservative positions), and this is true particularly of the idea of revelation in history, which is part of our subject today. As against the liberal idea of a gradual advancement to more elevated, spiritual, and universal ideas, revelation in history was a distinct improvement. But it was not properly observed that such things, though relatively justified when set against the liberal theology, were not thereby *absolutely* justified; nor were they made free from internal tensions which would later damage or destroy them.

Second, the period was one in which it was thought that the ultimate questions were those of total presuppositions and of sweeping, commanding synthetic assumptions. Get rid of non-biblical presuppositions, it was supposed, and your main problem would be gone. There were non-biblical presuppositions, which had to be rejected *en masse*; and there were biblical assumptions, which had to be stated and accepted in entirety. This was the atmosphere of the period. It began with a weariness and a hostility toward the sort of analysis which had dominated biblical study in the source-critical approach; and turning away from this it sought wide synthetic statements which would be valid for the Bible as a whole. It was not seen that these new concepts of biblical theology would be subject to, and would have to be subjected to, an analysis of quite another kind; indeed people learned to suppose that any sort of analytic approach was negative and destructive. As against this emphasis on general presuppositions and assumptions, I believe, and I think that this is clearly supported by the troubles that befell biblical theology and led to its eventual collapse, that the problem is rather one of logic, in the widest sense: what meanings do you attach to words, and how do you use them in the development of an argument? Biblical theology, because it was careless about this and despised it, fell too much into a kind of argumentation that I would call basically rhetorical rather than logical.

Two examples may be offered to illustrate this point. When, in the light of later developments, we look back at the influence of a book like Wright's *God Who Acts*, the fundamentally rhetorical character of its argumentation becomes clear. The supposed reassertion of biblical language as against systematic theology, propositional theology, and so on, is straight pulpit rhetoric. On the central issue, that of the ontological status of the acts of God, the rhetoric appeared to give full value to the realistic biblical language about God's dividing the sea, leading the Israelites out of Egypt, and so on. It left concealed the whole strongly historicistic and naturalistic attitude with which a man like Wright as a historian and archaeologist looked upon actual historical events; this attitude was left to make itself felt later and through different channels. The whole success and impact of the book depended on this rhetorical concealment of the logical issue. It was therefore a long time before the issue became clear.[5] This situation was not peculiar to this particular book; rather, it was the whole intellectual atmosphere of the biblical theology movement that permitted and approved this rhetorical approach and resisted the application of an analysis which would have broken it open.

Another example: the often-canvassed view that in ancient Israel words had 'power' in a sense foreign to our experience also rested on religious rhetoric and fell to pieces as soon as it was considered logically.[6] Of course one can find in the Old Testament instances of words, names, and sentences that are conceived of as having power, but it is quite unjustified to generalize this into the notion that all words, names, and sentences are so regarded. If they have power, it is because they are the words, names and sentences of powerful persons, like God or great kings, prophets, and commanders; no one in Israel thought that the word 'egg' or 'mud' conveyed the 'power' of eggs or of mud in any way beyond ways found equally among modern men.

Biblical theology, then, in the English-speaking world fell a victim to a rhetoric derived very often from traditional pulpit exposition. The Continental version of the same movement also suffered from rhetorical use of concepts, where analytic examination of them was much more needed. The language of Continental biblical theology was drawn from a more academic stratum and more associated with the mainstream of systematic theology – I think, for instance, of the function within von Rad's *Old Testament Theology* of terms like 'kerygma' or 'confession' (this latter will be mentioned again below). In general, however, we may sum up by reiterating the main point of this section: biblical theology encouraged the use of sweeping and wholesale dominant terms rather than the careful and analytic dissection of what they might mean in this connection or in that. At the worst, terms became slogans – rhetorical tokens which were used wildly and generally, with little care for precision or for distinctions in sense.

Third, biblical theology as it developed came to suffer from some severe inner contradictions and antinomies. These occurred on both a conceptual and a practical level. On the conceptual level I will shortly illustrate some antinomies that attended the concept of history, but when I speak of a practical level I mean this sort of thing: the fact that the best works written within biblical theology often substantially contradicted the emphases most beloved by the biblical theology movement as a whole. For instance, the emphasis of the movement as a whole was on the unity of the Bible and the search for one pervasive biblical theology, as against the differing religious concepts detected and differentiated for each source by historical criticism; but one of the finest Old Testament theologies, that of von Rad, denied at least in some senses that there was such a unity and asserted a plurality of different theologies within the Old Testament itself.[7] These then are a selection among the factors that led to the decline of biblical theology, or at least of biblical theology as it was. In the case of history as the medium or locus of revelation, as I have pointed out before, agreement on the abstract principle that history was central and all-important did nothing to prevent the appearance of deep oppositions and contradictions in the understanding of what this meant.[8] The difference between von Rad's position and that of Wright is a good example, to which we shall refer again later.[9]

With these prolegomena about the general position of biblical theology we can turn to a closer examination of the status of story and history. I do not have to explain that the idea of revelation through history was basic to most or all biblical theology in a period like 1945–60. It was in many ways the focal point of the entire idea of biblical theology and summarized its values: revelation through history was supposed to be charac-teristic of Hebrew thought, unknown to the Greeks, unknown to the rest of the extra-biblical world, common to the entire Bible and thus the underlying basis of its inner unity, unintel-ligible to philosophy, and poorly understood by theologians other than biblical theologians. In 1962 I gave a lecture at Prince-ton in which I questioned some of this; it was Martin E. Marty, former associate dean of the Divinity School here in Chicago, who was good enough to reprint that lecture in the first volume of his *New Theology* series[10] and give it wider circulation, and I would like to acknowledge that kindness here. But that lecture was only the beginning of a re-examination of the question, and today I want to carry it somewhat further. It was then perhaps somewhat adventurous to question the centrality of revelation in history, and the mere raising of the question necessitated the use of a fair amount of negative evidence. It was therefore not difficult to try to brush the argument aside as mere negative protest against the great positive thrust of modern theology,[11] and I do not know if even the good Mr Marty did not permit the word 'iconoclast' to appear in his editorial comment. Today, when the great positive thrust of biblical theology lies largely in ruins, and this largely as a consequence of the uncritical and unanalytic complacency of its practitioners, we can look at the question more calmly and start a new analysis more coolly. I propose therefore not to start with a critical analysis of older positions but with a positive statement of the sort of position I now think to be viable. After making this statement I shall go back over some of the points of controversy and difficulty.

Now the core of my position is already manifest in the title of this lecture. The long narrative corpus of the Old Testament seems to me, as a body of literature, to merit the title of story rather than that of history. Or, to put it in another way, it seems to merit entirely the title of story but only in part the title history; or, again, we may adopt the term used by Hans Frei and say that the narrative is 'history-like'.[12]

A moment may be spent on a terminological question. Story and history are different in English, but in German one uses *Geschichte* for both. This, however, like most of the language differences that so impressed biblical theology, is only a surface difference and not one lying in deep structure. If we have two terms, as in English, that is convenient, but it is not essential:

if one term, like *Geschichte*, is used, we simply ask that it be understood with the value that we attach in English to 'story'. This is indeed already often done in German exegesis, especially when a single story is intended, as in *die Elia-Geschichte*, and so on. The question is of a meaning rather than of a term. No one will question, however, that when *Geschichte* has been used as a general term and as a correlate of revelation in biblical theology its value has been that of history rather than that of story.[13]

Now biblical theology was quite right in referring to the central and dominant importance of the great mass of narrative material within the Old Testament. It was also quite right in asserting that the presence and the dominance of this material within the religious tradition made a quite decisive (though not an absolute) difference as against many other religious and cultural traditions that can be compared with it. But it was wrong in predicating history univocally of this material. What was sufficient and necessary was to assert that the narrative material, this story, had *certain* of the features that belong to history. For instance:

(*a*) The story is, broadly speaking, a unitary story, as distinct from separate anecdotes about people who might have lived at any time: the individual units are slotted into a total framework and have their function within the literary effect of the whole. You can illustrate this by contrast if you think of a story like that of Job, which stands outside of the framework, so that no one knows – at least so far as the story itself discloses – when Job lived or whether his experiences had any effect on anything else that happened. If, instead of the Pentateuch, we had twenty or thirty stories like Job, then the Bible would be a very different thing. The story is unitary and cumulative.

(*b*) The story is provided with a chronological framework which sets it against a time scale. The story marks all major events from the absolute date of the creation of the world, and from time to time it also gives crude but significant synchronisms against what was understood to be going on in other nations, like the Edomites or Moabites.

(*c*) Certain segments of the story constitute a fairly reliable *source* of historical evidence for the period in which the narrative is set. That is to say, these segments describe events in such a way that the description constitutes evidence from which (in combination with evidence from other sources) the modern historian can reconstruct a historical picture of the period. The degree of this reliability varies, however, from one segment to another.

(*d*) Certain segments of the story can be counted as coming close in certain respects to actual history writing. This is a different thing from the one mentioned just above, although the two are commonly confused. We here mean not only that the narrative contains evidence that can be used with some confidence by the modern historian but also that the writer himself had some of the attributes of a historian. While this can be validly asserted, with suitable qualification, of some segments within the story, it cannot be applied to the story as a whole or to the Old Testament as a whole.

All these are ways in which the narrative material of the Old Testament can be associated with history. But against this we have to set aspects in which it differs from history.

(*a*) The story contains within itself large elements which no one seriously considers as history and which belong rather to the area of myth and legend (for our present purpose it is not important to differentiate between these two). This includes the entire (and supremely important) primeval story: creation, the angel marriages, Noah and the flood, and so on. But we cannot confine myth and legend to those sections which are purely and absolutely of this character: it is likely to include a lot of further material running all through the patriarchal period and indeed right down through the later story to the end of the kingdom. Indeed, rather than say that the dominance of history is characteristic of the Old Testament, it would be more correct to say that what is characteristic is its peculiarly blended mixture of historical (or partly historical) narration with mythical and legendary elements. Thus:

(*b*) The story moves back and forward, quite without embarrassment, between human causation and divine causation, between the statement and description of events in entirely human terms (no doubt with theological aims, purposes, and overtones, but still in entirely human terms) and the statement of events in a fashion utilizing express and large-scale divine intervention. The ability to mingle these styles is a mark of the genius of the literature, but it is also a sign that history is not a governing factor in the selection and presentation of material.

(*c*) Within the narrative literature other forms of motivation than the historical can easily be detected. I content myself here

with citing the discussion by R. Smend, in which he separates
out the 'aetiological' and the 'paradigmatic' as two modes in
which the 'mythical' thinking of Israel flows into the 'historical'
writing.[14] Aetiology gives an explanation, set in the past, of
how something came to be as it now is. The paradigmatic
provides analogies in which experience, past or future, can be
understood and expressed. Neither of these is really historical
in original basis and motivation, but the narrative literature is
full of both.

(*d*) The telling of the story in the Old Testament is devoid of
one element that seems essential for history as we understand
the term, namely, some critical evaluation of sources and
reports. Considering the important place that historical reporting takes within the Judaeo-Christian tradition, it was fateful
for the later development of the religions concerned that their
canonical literature never included this element of critical questioning, which is already present in the first beginnings of Greek
historiography with Herodotus. Because the biblical documents
lacked this critical-historical sense, it became possible and natural that the critical examination of historical reports could not
establish itself within the stream of Judaeo-Christian tradition
until a late stage, and the process is still incomplete today.

Thus, to sum up the argument so far, the story has two great
characteristics. First, it is cumulative. Starting from the beginning, it sketches in more and more of the background for the
stages that are to come and provides the essential assumptions
for the understanding of them. Second, it spirals back and
forward across history, sometimes coming closer to it, sometimes going farther away from it. Thus it is essential that the
story is a unitary and cumulative story; it is also essential that
it has *some* contact with history, but that contact is tangential
and partial rather than systematic and complete.

Now I should give a moment to one or two possible objections
at this point. It may be said – and this was a characteristic
biblical theology argument – that I have assumed we know
what we mean by the word 'history'. Is it not 'positivism' –
widely rumoured to be a bad thing – to suppose that it is not
history if we describe events through the agency of divine
causality? I do not consider this to be a serious argument.
History means only what we mean by our use of the word
'history'. Theoretically one might suppose that the Bible, suitably interrogated, might reveal another kind of 'history' which

would then have precedence over what we mean by the word. But there is no reason to start on that procedure until we have first of all demonstrated that history is the appropriate term with which to commence operations, and I have just shown reasons why this is not so.

Again, it may be argued that the view just expressed assumes that God does not act in history and does not affect it. It assumes nothing of the sort. It simply observes that we do not apply the term 'history' to a form of investigation which resorts to divine agency as a mode of explanation.

Again, it is true that there are many different views among historians and theoreticians of history about what constitutes history. This is so but for my purpose it does not matter. What I say applies on the assumption of any of these different views. There is no intellectually serious conception of history – except among what remains of the tradition of biblical theology, and even there maintained only in forms that are equivocal and disingenuous – that would allow us to classify all the narrative material of the Old Testament, or even most of it, as 'history'.

We are now in a position to make a preliminary 'placing' of the biblical story in relation to the two forms of historical operation that come most closely in contact with it. We can usefully deploy three elements, as follows:

(*a*) First, the story, as told in the narrative literature of the Old Testament, a massive literary form, made up from many sources but having its own integrity and consistency in the midst of multitudinous differences.

(*b*) The history of the period in Israel (or should we not rather say in Palestine, and beyond that in the wider Near Eastern environment?), that is, the sequence of external events as it may be reconstructed by historians and archaeologists.

(*c*) The history of tradition which culminated in the formation of the biblical text. Like the history of Israel or of Palestine, this is not plainly set forth on the surface of the text and has to be reconstructed by historical methods; but in a sense it can be deemed 'internal' to the formation of the Bible, while the political and general history is external.

Now, between these different elements the emphasis of scholarship can fall in different ways. For the present purpose I am emphasizing the story itself, not because this is the only way of looking at things but because an emphasis on the story is the element in my thinking that corresponds to what in the older biblical theology would have been called an emphasis on history or on revelation through history, in other words, the issue from which we began.

We can usefully illustrate this by comparing two different approaches made familiar within biblical theology. First, a typical American expression of biblical theology within the Albrightian tradition, as exemplified by Wright. This approach utilized the story character of the material in order to establish and validate the revelatory function of 'history' or of 'events', but once this was done tended to pass quickly over to the external history (*b* above). Although this approach laid enormous emphasis upon the events, which emphasis was grounded upon characteristics of the narrative form of the Old Testament story, it thereafter gave comparatively little attention to the actual narrative form of Old Testament literature – necessarily so, since the actual character of the events, as understood, was far remote from the way in which they are described in detail in the text.[15] On the other hand, the treatment of the external history (*b* above) tended to assume a conservative character, as if the revelatory character of the biblical narrative encouraged, justified, or even required a maximum assessment of its reporting accuracy, when taken as evidence for external history.

A typical and central Continental position, by contrast, is that of von Rad. His approach to the story is far more closely connected with the form of the text and with exegesis than one can find in the Albrightian tradition – Albright and his followers seem to have had, on the whole, no feeling for a text as literature with its meaning in itself; they read it as a collection of pieces of evidence from which, on the model of archaeological study, historical stages might be reconstructed. But, though von Rad has a fine literary sense for the story, his approach to the theological explication of the text comes primarily through the history of tradition (our *c* above). But then the model upon which the history of tradition is conceived is a peculiar one; it is something like a creed, a short and summary statement of salient events, *credenda*, to which a prime theological value is attached. The development of tradition is conceived as being governed by such a principle: the full tradition is generated, as it were, by and from this basic creed. The von Rad theology, though deeply imaginative, poetic, and sensitive to the currents of Old Testament thinking in a way quite foreign to the Albright-Wright approach, develops several serious antinomies.

First of all, it leads directly to the appearance of two 'histories', one the history 'confessed' by Israel, which according to von Rad is the basis for Old Testament theology, the other the history reconstructed by critical scholarship.[16] It is, I submit, an ultimately impossible position to argue that revelation is in history but that it has to be understood on the basis of the confessed history rather than on that of critical history. Second, not all of the story told in the Old Testament, 'history' in von Rad's terms, counts for him as 'salvation history'. For instance, so huge and impressive a segment as the story of David, paradoxically by the opinion of many scholars one of the most truly 'historical' parts of the story in the sense of being both a reliable historical source and a document written with something of a true historiographical purpose and motivation, does not count as salvation history because it is not part of the basic creed.[17] Third, a point to which we shall return, the von Rad theology has insuperable problems with the later stages of the Old Testament as a whole. Because in post-exilic times thinking changes, and in particular the emphasis on history is reduced, von Rad cannot accommodate these late developments within the system of values that he has used and so is forced, as so many other Old Testament theologians have been, to treat them as a degeneration.[18]

Thus, to summarize, in both of these widely received forms of biblical theology the story character of the Old Testament narrative, when identified as 'history' and then allowed to expand into senses of that word other than those that are justified by that story character, has led to severe antinomies and difficulties.

We reiterate. What I have called story is an absolutely essential and central aspect of the Old Testament; it cannot, however, be too simply identified, indeed it cannot be identified at all, with history.[19] Story belongs to literary form and cannot be removed from it without danger. First, the sequence of the story follows literary form: the story builds up cumulatively from the beginning and its unity as a story, being dependent on the bonds provided by the sequence and on the links indicated by the chronological scheme and the synchronisms, has its reference point in the beginning. From a certain point of view, indeed, it may be possible to suppose (I do not grant this, but am willing to suppose it) that the early story takes its beginnings from a credal statement generated from the exodus, but even if the Israelite theological tradition has developed in this way it does not mean that the Pentateuch is meant to be read in that way.[20] It is meant to be read not as the reflection of forces in the history of tradition which brought it into being but as a story developing and unfolding from its own beginning.

Second, the character of the story belongs to literary form. As a young American scholar addressing the Albrightian point of view has recently put it, rather crudely and brutally but with pungent expressiveness: 'Salvation history did not happen; it is a literary form which has its own historical context.'[21]

Third, the character of some segments of the story cannot be explained as generated out of Israelite-Yahwistic theology alone. The earlier story, and elements here and there in the later, are in part clearly inherited from ancient Near Eastern sources. Rather than thinking of a core of Israelite theology which gradually shaped and generated the material, controlling it from the beginning, we have to think of an Israelite religion which gradually separated itself out of the mass of Near Eastern material and which only at a relatively late date began to impose itself through organizing formulations of credal character.

With this we pass to one of the themes traditional in all discussion of the place of story and history. The now traditional claim that the Old Testament is uniquely a work of historical thinking was always supported by the assertion that other contemporary or comparable cultures had no understanding of history, set no value upon history, and so on. How does this claim appear in the light of a decade of rethinking?

It was always absurd of biblical theology to claim that 'the Greeks' saw no significance in history. Why, if so, did they write so much of it? Moreover, out of the total construct history with which we operate, and upon which so much value has been set in biblical theology, there are some important constituents for which the intellectual ancestry is entirely Hellenic: in particular, the critical question, already mentioned above, whether sources and reports are reliable or not, a kind of enquiry which is entirely lacking in the Judeo-Christian tradition until quite late times. And if one goes further, as some have done, and admits that the Greeks of course wrote plenty of history but that only the Hebrews saw theological significance in it, this also is quite disputable. Perhaps we may cite Roman historiography rather than Greek, for Roman in a number of ways presents a more suitable comparison with Israelite writing.

Livy's history of Rome can well be construed as expressing on a grand scale the favour of the gods to the people of Rome, and Virgil's version of the travels of Aeneas from Troy to Latium was certainly a theological legitimation of the Augustan principate. One may certainly claim with assurance that the place of the biblical narrative within Israelite culture was quite different from the role that any historical work had within the culture of the Greeks or of the Romans; but to phrase this as if 'history' itself belonged to Israel rather than to the Greco-Roman world must now be considered only as one of the more bizarre aberrations from reason within the older biblical theology.[22] It is interesting that the creative young German Old Testament scholar, R. Smend, can now cite with some measure of approval the words written by W. Vatke, one of the fathers of Pentateuchal criticism, in 1835:

> The Hebrews did not at all raise themselves to the standpoint of properly historical contemplation, and there is no book of the Old Testament, however much it may contain material that is otherwise objectively historical, that deserves the name of true historiography.[23]

It is, Smend suggests, only apologetic motives that would make it easy to contradict this. But who would have dared to repeat such a remark, with any measure of consent or approval, fifteen years ago?

What then about the Near Eastern background? Here too things have altered. It used to be thought and asserted that divine action in history was unique to Israel, while in the environing nations the religion was one of nature alone and not of history. But this view, familiar as it has been in the work of theologians, seems to me to have its origin in Western philosophical ideas going back long before anything precise was known about ancient Near Eastern religions. An important article by H. Gese in 1958 already showed that significant moves toward a historical viewpoint were being made in the ancient Near East before the rise of Israel;[24] and in 1967 B. Albrektson's book *History and the Gods* shows clearly that the gods of other nations had also 'acted in history':

> The Old Testament idea of historical events as divine revelation must be counted among the similarities, not among the distinctive traits: it is part of the common theology of the ancient Near East.[25]

No more shattering blow against the older biblical theology

could be imagined.[26] It is true that some significant criticism of
Albrektson's book has been made by competent Orientalists;
but I shall not attempt here either to repeat or to rebut those
criticisms.[27] What seems to me important, within our present
subject, is this: even the criticisms of Albrektson's work are
almost as destructive of the traditional position as his book itself
had been. Let me quote the distinguished Assyriologist W. G.
Lambert:[28]

> The basic differences between the Hebrew and the ancient Meso-
> potamian ideas of destiny and divine intervention in human affairs
> spring from their contrasting monotheism and polytheism.

Quite so. Lambert is not quite satisfied with Albrektson's iden-
tification of divine action in history as a common element. He
does not dispute this in itself, but thinks that a view of the
wider setting would show distinctivenesses between Israel and
Mesopotamia – and I do not see that Albrektson would necessarily disagree with this. But Lambert's criticism moves the discussion on to other ground altogether. The foundation for the
distinctiveness of Israel lies no longer in divine action in history.
Rather, it lies in the idea of God, and in particular in the idea
of the one God as against the many gods of other nations and
cultures – an opposition the importance of which is amply
supported by the Old Testament itself. But, if this is so, far
from divine action in history providing a foundation for the
perception of God, it may be that the peculiar perception of
God was the foundation for the idea of divine action as the
biblical story depicts it.[29] But with this the entire balance of
received biblical theology, predicated upon revelation in history
as the point of origin, is overturned.[30] The distinctiveness of
Israelite faith cannot be predicated uniquely upon the significance of history but depends on the total organization of thinking and religion.

With this we may pass to one other question, which was
either neglected or answered in an unsatisfactory way in the
older biblical theology. What happened to the characteristic Old
Testament story form (in biblical theology terms, to salvation
history) at the end of the Old Testament period? If the Old
Testament developed to a very high point the use of narrative
as a form for theological expression, it seems also to have
brought that same development to some kind of an end. By
about the time when Christianity arose, the situation was more

or less the reverse of that which has been taken as typical. Historiographical productivity on really pure Jewish soil was very thin, and it was where Jewish life was in contact with the Greek historiographical tradition that it was productive in historical writing. The Qumran documents include no historical writings. In many major currents of Judaism what I have here called story, unitary and cumulative, broke down into anecdote and annotation. The sense of temporal distance was lost, for in much rabbinic discourse persons of remote antiquity are depicted as living and thinking in the terms of Tannaitic rabbis. What had now happened to revelation in history? Von Rad is frank in making explicit what most biblical theologians have merely implied – it had more or less come to a stop.[31] Very well – but the blame for this – and within the categories and values of most biblical theology it is very blameworthy indeed, for no offence is more serious than the loss from sight of salvation history – cannot reasonably be shunted off on to post-biblical developments. If such a change took place the responsibility cannot be placed upon a sort of degeneration that occurred in post-biblical Judaism, for it was the central redaction of the Old Testament itself that basically caused the change. Those who laud the Old Testament for having made history central to theological expression will also have to censure it for having done much to stifle this same movement.

I would express it in a different way. The story that is central to so much of the Old Testament gradually became a completed story. There were some ragged ends, it is true, but basically it rounded itself off, with one great stage describing the process down to the death of Moses – and this stage stated in story form the establishment of the Jewish polity of post-exilic times – and another describing it from Moses down to the end of the kingdom and the return from exile. The completion of the story lets it fall into the past. Its falling into the past, and its recognition as holy scripture and thus as qualitatively superior to any other story, means that all future tradition has to take another form. The whole catastrophic picture suggested by von Rad's view just quoted, the picture of a perception fed upon salvation history which then suddenly descended into the abyss of a non-historical perspective, can thus be avoided. But it cannot be avoided so long as 'history' is taken as the ultimate and absolute value for a theological understanding of the Old Testament.[32]

Let us now go back to our three layers of material, or our

three modes of considering and reading the material: the story itself, which constitutes a very large segment of the Old Testament; the history of tradition from which the Old Testament grew; and the history of culture, society, and politics which formed the context for them all. Where in all this, in the terms that the older biblical theology would have used, does revelation lie?

Now to this question there is no single or simple answer. In one very central sense I would say that the basic revelation of God, in the sense of the initiation of communication between God and man, is not in the Bible, nor narrated in the Bible, but is presupposed by the Bible. From the beginning it assumes that you know who God is and that he is in communication with man. Unlike the situation in modern theology, there is thus no problem of revelation which has to be solved or overcome. The whole society, and not only the Yahwistic theology, assumes that you can talk with God and hear him and receive the knowledge of his will. What you learn about God in the Bible is not the first contact with deity, it is new information about a person whom you already know. But in another way it can be said that the Bible is the locus of revelation, for it is the expression which the Israelite tradition has in fact formed, the way in which it wants to speak on the basis of that which it has heard and learned. This would imply that the reading of the story is the way to meet the God whom they met; and this might mean that the explication of the story for itself, as a story, is the right form for a biblical theology.[33] But if the Bible is the expression of Israelite tradition, is not the growth of the tradition, rather than the story itself, the area where the actual dynamics of revelation are to be seen? Well, again, yes, for this is an entirely justifiable approach. In this case we can say that the locus of revelation is not the Old Testament, the book; it is rather Israel, the people, Israel in its historical experience in a certain period.[34] This approach entirely justifies the grounding of a theology upon the history of tradition as well as its taking full account of the general social and political history. Yet Israel in its historical experience in the biblical period is not something congruent with what Israel presented and expressed in its story and in the rest of the canonical literature; it is the story, and the Bible as a whole, that is Israel's expression of what it wanted to say. It seems then that there is no single locus which uniquely represents the core to which theological investigation aspires to attain; we have therefore a justification for a multiple approach, but also good reason for better discrimination between elements that are discerned through one approach and those that are discerned through another.

What is the result of all this for biblical theology? Our study suggests that it is not so very difficult to make a fresh analysis of the concepts involving story and history in a way that can both do justice to the valid emphases which biblical theology sought to maintain and at the same time avoid some of the antinomies and contradictions into which it fell. This in turn raises the question whether it was necessary for biblical theology to run into such great trouble and decline as it did: Was the concept of a biblical theology in itself utterly wrong and therefore doomed to self-destruction, or was it only mishandled in the execution? Present trends, in spite of the great misfortunes of the subject in the last ten or fifteen years, suggest two things: first of all, that it expressed and concerned itself with elements of vital theological importance which would almost certainly be neglected or badly treated if there were no such thing as biblical theology at all; and, second, that the healing of the wounds, often self-inflicted, of biblical theology is not an insuperable task. We can close therefore upon a note of hopefulness for our theme.

2

Does Biblical Study Still Belong to Theology?

The question, whether biblical study still belongs to theology, would at one time, indeed not very long ago, have been regarded as an eccentric one. Until the last one or two decades it would have seemed to most people obvious that the study of the Bible was part of the total academic and ecclesiastical enterprise known as theology. The academic study of the Bible within universities was part of the curriculum of the faculty of theology. Theology as a subject was studied mainly – indeed, almost exclusively – by persons intending to seek ordination in the ministry of the various churches; and the tutors and professors who instructed them were similarly men who had come from, and indeed were still within, the ordained ministry of these churches. And today something of this situation still survives, the degree of its survival varying from country to country and from one social situation to another.

Nevertheless a substantial displacement of emphasis has taken place. Purely as a matter of educational practice and policy, biblical study is no longer necessarily undertaken within the bosom of the theological enterprise in this sense. On the contrary, the term 'biblical study', or more commonly 'biblical studies' in the plural, is now often used to designate a department in a university, or a course, that is not part of the theological faculty but undertakes the teaching of the Bible, its text, its languages, its history, and indeed its religion and theology, as a subject in its own right, understood to possess a wholeness and integrity comparable with that which is found in the study of (say) classics, or French, or English. Competent students and teachers of biblical subjects who have never studied the traditional comprehensive field of theology, and who have never contemplated ordination to the ministry, are becoming less and less rare. And even within faculties of theology in the traditional sense, which encompass the entire field of traditional theological subjects, there has been an increasing influx of students who not only do not intend to seek ordination but who have no religious commitment at all and who are thus studying the subject as a general humanistic education, just as one might study Greek civilization or social anthropology. It is thus not surprising if there now appears to be some question just how biblical study is related to theology, and particularly to theology conceived of as a rounded and comprehensive scheme of preparation for entry into the holy ministry.

Now it is not my purpose in this lecture to follow out the implications of this on the level of educational policy or of the departmental structure of universities; as I shall shortly show, my main interest lies in the inner philosophy, so to speak, of modern biblical study, rather than in the organizational implications of it. Nevertheless I cannot resist the temptation to include at this point some remarks about problems of educational policy and about the general position of biblical interpretation within our modern culture.

First of all, theology, in the sense of the body of material studied within a comprehensive theological faculty, is not a single subject in the sense in which economics, or philosophy, or English, is a single subject. Rather, it is a constellation of different fields and subjects held together by the fact that they are studied as they relate to God, to the church, its work and its tradition, and to the Bible. There is thus no one specific theological method or methodology that covers all the ground: on the contrary, the methods are in large measure drawn from principles of method already standard within history, within literary criticism, within linguistics, within philosophy, within psychology and social studies, and these are applied as is appropriate to much of the material that is agreed to come within the purview of a faculty of theology.

This means that within theological studies, taken as a whole, there is often a powerful tug between one subject and another. Time spent on Hebrew seems to be time taken away from doctrinal theology, and time spent on social and practical theology competes with time devoted to the New Testament. This would perhaps not matter if the course of studies in theology was a lengthy one; but, as we know, it is not a lengthy one. On the whole, as the diversity and complexity of the matter has been increasing, the effective length of courses in theology in many centres has been decreasing. Only a few decades ago, even if courses were not longer, they assumed as a starting requirement a thorough command of Greek, which now has to be begun by many at university level, and even of Hebrew. The vocational aspect of a course in theology, with its very proper emphasis on present-day problems and on the interpretation of the church's message for the man of today, pulls against the command of subjects like biblical languages, which are the foundation of serious study of the church's own scriptures. It may be otherwise perhaps in an educational system such as that of the United States, where it is often understood that a first degree provides only an introduction to a subject and that real education in it begins only at the post-graduate level. For many of us in this country this option is not available. The average course in theology, containing a component of biblical study, can no longer in normal circumstances provide an advanced education in scripture comparable with what is normal in fields like classics or philosophy, or even in language subjects commonly begun at university level such as Russian or Arabic. I do not say these things in order to argue that a larger share of the theology cake should be devoured by the study of the Bible. As far as this present argument goes, there may be perfectly good reasons within theology why the balance of education must be as it is. I simply argue that, in such measure as theology comes to emphasize present-day problems and modern philosophical debate, in that same measure it makes it likely that the centre of technical and advanced biblical studies will move away from theology. Thus theological education itself by its own inner pressures may perhaps contribute to the independence of biblical study as an academic subject. Already a very important contribution to the understanding of the Bible is coming from faculties and departments of classics, ancient history, Assyriology, Semitic linguistics, Jewish studies and other such subjects, and the extent and importance of this contribution may well be expected to increase.

Now to avoid misunderstanding, I want to make it clear that the essential difference is not that between a church-related theological faculty on the one side and a department or faculty in a modern secular university on the other, as if in the former case it were agreed that biblical study is part of general theology and in the latter that it had nothing to do with theology. People may sometimes speak in that way but things seem to work out in a more complex manner. It could not be said that the study of scripture in secular institutions has been productive of strongly secular or irreligious understandings of it. On the contrary, comparatively little secularistic interpretation of scripture has been emerging from the biblical scholarship of such institutions, at least in our country, and we have certainly had nothing to compare with the expressly non-theological, let us say Marxist, interpretation of the Bible that is to be found in some continental countries. The actual tendency has been in the opposite direction: biblical studies in our modern universities have often tended to offer a shelter for a traditional and conservative religiosity in interpretation, such as would have been approved by an older-fashioned religious current but would not have stood up against the acid scrutiny of modern theological discussion, informed by the full tradition of the church's thinking in modern times. When the high priest of our modern popular culture, the television interviewer, wants someone to argue that Jesus never existed or that nothing definite can be known about him, it is seldom that the professor of biblical studies in a modern university can be found to do this for him. I would not be surprised if our ancient universities, with their comprehensive faculties of theology, harbour a more sceptical spirit in their thought about the Bible than the modern secular universities with their less theological approach. This may seem paradoxical but paradoxes are often profoundly true.

There are thus two different issues here. The first is an issue of educational organization: to sum up, educational conditions may in the future favour an increasing independence of academic biblical studies from theology. The second, and for my purpose the more important, is an issue that lies within the mind of the biblical scholar himself: how far must he think and work, and how far does he think and work, in terms that are really theological?

At this point we have to make a more precise definition of what is meant by the term 'theological'. Thus far I have used the term in a very general sense, as a comprehensive designator for all the matter that is taught or treated of in theological faculties. But much of this matter can be adequately described also as history, linguistics, sociology and so on. Is there any matter that can be described as essentially and specifically theological?

In order to elucidate this, we can perhaps distinguish two elementary logical forms. The first is the form 'God is X', or, in other words, 'We believe that God is X', 'We ought to affirm that God is X.' The second is the form: 'This or that biblical writer said, or thought, that God is X.' The first is a statement of personal faith, or a statement of the church's faith: it is a theological statement in the strict sense. The second is a descriptive statement: perhaps historical, perhaps structural, perhaps falling under some other category, but in any case a descriptive statement. The first is a statement which, however closely related to evidence, is not merely an interpretation of evidence: its logic is not exhaustively explained by stating the evidence to which it may relate itself. The second is an interpretation of given evidence. Theology in the stricter sense involves the use of assertions having the first form: this is what the church says in its creeds and its worship, it is what the individual believer says, and it is what the theologian says. But a great deal of academic biblical study seems to take the second form: it does not say what God is, it reports on what the biblical texts say about him. If theology in the strict sense makes assertions about the divine, biblical study seems a great deal of the time to make assertions about human relations. But is this enough or is it not enough? Our original question, 'Does biblical study still belong to theology?' can thus be translated into this other terminology: 'Do judgments of the second form also imply judgments of the first form?' Or: 'In order to make judgments of the second form in an adequate and comprehensive way, sufficiently covering the material of the Bible, does the scholar also have to make judgments of the first form?' Does the biblical scholar have to be, in *this* sense, a theologian? This seems to be the centre of the question.

At first sight it seems that the answer is in the negative. Modern biblical scholarship appears to initiate one into a world of discourse which indeed has contacts with that of theology and which overlaps with the world of theology but which nevertheless does not belong to it, in the sense of being at any point absolutely dependent on it. It is a world in which scholars of one theological position and those of another, and those who have no theological position at all, exist together as colleagues and consider one another's positions, somewhat independently of the fact that this scholar or that may hold such and such theological views, or indeed profess to hold no theological views at all. My own experience as an Old Testament scholar can be formulated in one central observation: although I know personally most of the Old Testament scholars of my generation, and know their works and the sort of ideas they represent, in very many cases I do not know what sort of theology they believe in, or if I know it I know it by the way, through a sort of incidental process of guessing and deducing from odd hints here and there; if I know it at all, it is not because the giving of information about one's theological beliefs is any structurally essential part of modern biblical scholarship. On the other hand, all Old Testament scholars in the main currents of scholarship are aware of the great overlap between the work of those who are also theologically motivated, who want to say something in my first form, something that affirms faith in God, and those who do not want to say anything of the sort at all. It seems that the methods of biblical study are a mixture of the methods of history, of linguistics, of literary interpretation and of the history of religion, but that theology in the strict sense is optional rather than necessary. Thus, we may ask, just as a century and a half ago theology lost control over geology and palaeontology, have biblical studies in the end also escaped from its dominion?

Now one of the ways in which the independence of biblical studies is most often asserted is through the claim of objectivity. The study of scripture, it is said, ought to be based upon factual observation alone. Theological conviction will often seek to override the factual data, and this means that theology is a distorting influence within the study of scripture. The way to cure this, it is thought, is to keep the study of scripture strictly separate from the considerations and the influences of theology. This may seem to be a rather anti-theological point of view and yet it may be claimed, in defence of it, that it is only a logical extension of what theologians themselves often say. For the theologian himself often says of someone: his theological convictions are such that he cannot appreciate what the Bible itself is actually saying. Thus the demand for objectivity, for an appreciation of the data in themselves and in distinction to theological hypotheses about them, is not in itself an anti-theological position but is one inherent in the structure of theological thought itself. And surely rightly so. Some trends in modern theology, especially trends influenced by existentialism, justifiably troubled by what they saw as the dry and unexciting objectivism of the modern lecture-room, have reacted by tending to belittle the virtue of objectivity and to suggest that it is not a gift to be much prized. Surely this reaction has been mistaken, and at its worst it has opened the floodgates to a propagandist misuse of the truth. Though theology can distort and damage objectivity, as theologians themselves continually admit, strong theological conviction can coexist with and rejoice in a very high degree of objectivity. It is true that complete objectivity is not attainable, but a high degree of objectivity is attainable, and a high degree of it is very much better than a low degree. And I venture to claim that shining examples of it can be found among my predecessors in the Oriel Professorship of the Interpretation of Holy Scripture. I think particularly of my immediate predecessor, Dr Sparks, surely a churchman if ever there was one and a man of deep and balanced theological conviction, who for considerable periods combined the duties of the professorship with the practical cure of souls in a variety of parishes, but whose scholarship was particularly devoted to that aspect in which objectivity is most essential and is yet attainable only through the most exacting and painstaking labour, namely the study of the text, especially that of the Greek and Latin Bibles. Before him I think of D. C. Simpson, who collected and published the volume of lectures on the Psalms (*The Psalmists*, 1926), which among English-language publications marked more than any other the turn towards the modern appreciation of Israel's sacred poetry; and before him of C. F. Burney, whose sober and careful commentary on the book of Judges (1918) is still esteemed by many as the best available single commentary on that book. To these should be added G. A. Cooke, whose *Textbook of North-Semitic Inscriptions* (1903) remained, because of its accuracy and reliability, the standard work on the subject for an unusually long time: only after a span of sixty to seventy years were efforts made to replace it. These have been men for whom personal theological commitment has gone hand in hand with, and has stimulated and supported, a strong commitment to objective and sober handling of the evidence.

The idea, then, that objectivity in biblical study can be attained through the exclusion of theological interest should not be accepted; and, as theologians have often and rightly pointed out, where theological interest has been excluded it has often been only to make room for some secular or pseudo-theological ideology which is equally destructive of objectivity. Clearly, the question cannot be settled through an absolute excluding of this or a wholesale permitting of that: rather, it is a question of the *quality* of a theological attitude which will encourage the biblical material to speak for itself, even against the current of prevailing theological opinions, and on the other side the *quality* of a non-theological biblical study which will nevertheless have sufficient openness of mind to permit theological questions to be asked. Theologians are right when they say, as they often do, that if theology is excluded from academic study of the Bible it will only mean one of two things: either that certain questions will not be asked at all, or that some other metaphysical assumption will rush in to fill the vacuum. The former of these alternatives, I think, is actually more prevalent than the latter. Experience suggests that certain levels and dimensions of scripture are not explored except when scholars are prepared, even if only as a hypothesis for the sake of argument, to think theologically, to ask the question, how would it be if this were really true of God? Or, to take a simple illustration from another sphere, from philosophy, how much would the study of an ancient thinker like Plato have been impoverished if throughout the ages scholars had confined themselves to expounding the text and its internal semantic linkages and had rigorously excluded from their minds the question 'Is Plato right?' ?

In this respect, then, we may hope to have justified the freedom of theological thought to be active within the study of scripture. But before we go further we have to look critically at two other arguments which theologians often propound. These arguments go a good deal further than we ourselves have gone: taken seriously, they would seem not only to justify the possibility of theological involvement within biblical study but to deny the possibility of non-theological study of the Bible.

The first is an argument about personal involvement. It is said that biblical study must not be pursued with cold detachment, as if it made no difference what the scholar's personal relation to the material might be. The material must be approached with empathy, and what more natural form of empathy than that which would be generated by the existential conviction that the biblical text is speaking 'for me', that it is thus in some way God's word for the scholar himself? The Bible must be read within the context of the church and of the church's faith, itself grounded upon these same scriptures.

This argument, however, goes too far. What it claims about empathy and personal involvement is indeed in itself right. The study of any subject is impoverished if these are absent. But empathy and personal involvement are not to be identified with the *acceptance* of the theological or ideological position of the matter studied. If this were strictly so, it would lead to an impossibly solipsistic position, and this is in fact characteristic of some tendencies in modern theology which have pressed this argument rather hard. It would mean that no one could express a valid opinion about a theology or a philosophy unless they were themselves adherents of that opinion. Theologians themselves of course do not at all conform to this ideal: they feel free to express judgments about (shall we say) gnosticism, without being in the slightest convinced of the validity of that intellectual system. Empathy with, and the understanding and appreciation of, a religious position are, though not easy, nevertheless perfectly attainable, on the level of the history of religions, or the comparative study of religions, or whatever we call it. Thus the argument from the need for empathy cannot be made to apply exclusively to theology and cannot demonstrate that all study of scripture *must* imply strictly theological involvement. Where the argument is valid is in its relation to such biblical study as is in fact theological: that is to say, when the study of scripture is undertaken as a theological task, then it must be done in the context of the church and with a personal involvement related to that context. But this does not prove that no valid biblical study can be undertaken except in that context.

The second such argument is about presuppositions. No kind of study, it is said, operates without presuppositions; and it is a vain hope that biblical study might be carried out without such presuppositions also. From this premise, jumping a wide gap, people go on to suggest that theology is the discipline which is in a position to examine and criticize the presuppositions of the biblical scholar or, in an even stronger form of the argument, to provide him with the correct presuppositions. The biblical scholar, it is implied, has theological or quasi-theological presuppositions in fact, but may conceal them from himself and from others. An express relationship with theology enables these presuppositions to be disclosed and thus (somehow) enables biblical study to be better directed towards its object.

Now this argument calls attention to a real fact, namely that biblical scholars tend to leave undiscussed the underlying presuppositions of their work. This may be true, but it does not in turn demonstrate either (*a*) that their work would be better, or of more service to theology, if these presuppositions were given more thorough discussion or (*b*) that theology, as theology, is in any better position to uncover, discuss or validate these presuppositions. In fact, where the biblical scholar learns more about the presuppositions of his work, this learning does not come from theology in the strict sense: it comes rather from logic and philosophy, from other sciences such as history and sociology, and most of all from the history of ideas, including the history of the past interpretation of the Bible and the history of theology itself. The theologian who identifies and analyses the presuppositions of biblical study does so not because of his theology as such but because, in comparison with biblical scholars, theologians are generally much better informed about the *later* history of ideas, just as the biblical specialist is better informed about the earlier. There is thus a diversity of information and of service, which should be duly recognized, but this constitutes no reason why theology as such should or must form the necessary intellectual context of biblical study.

Moreover, even from the viewpoint of theology itself it is doubtful whether the emphasis on the presuppositions of biblical study is salutary. Let us fully grant that the uncovering of presuppositions can be wholesome and stimulating. It does not follow from this that the structure of biblical study can be positively built upon a presuppositional foundation. Presuppositional criticism is essentially negative. It can help us to understand how and why certain wrong turns in the discipline have taken place; it does not tell us how to do it rightly. The fact, already admitted, that biblical scholars are not endlessly at work discussing their presuppositions is not necessarily a sign that they are at fault: it may be a significant pointer in another direction, an indication that the study of scripture is built in another way. The fact is that no one can advance or establish an opinion within biblical study on the grounds that he has the right presuppositions. He may have or he may not have, but in itself this tells us nothing: it provides no methods and it validates no conclusions. The science does not work in this way. A viewpoint expressed by a biblical scholar stands or falls, not by the relation between his opinion and his presuppositions, but by the relation between his opinion and the evidence.

We can put this in yet another way. It is in the interest of theology that it should allow and encourage the scripture to speak freely to the church and to theology. It must be able to say something other than what current theological and interpretative fashion would have it to say. But it cannot do this if theology controls the presuppositions with which it may be approached. It is thus in the interests of theology itself that the meaning of scripture should be allowed an adequate measure of independence; and that must mean that the discipline of biblical study also should be recognized to have a fitting independence.

I believe, then, that I have shown the inadequacy of each of the two extreme positions, on the one side the view that objectivity is to be gained through the exclusion of theological considerations from biblical study, and on the other side the view that the understanding of the Bible is not at all possible except through theological modes of understanding. Where then does the true position lie? It lies, I suggest, in the recognition that the study of scripture is a very complex operation involving many different levels and many different modes of operation. Certain of these levels – let us call them, without disparagement, the lower levels – can be studied and are studied only by operations normal to disciplines like historical study or linguistics. They require, indeed, an understanding of the cultural setting of the Bible, which is above all a religious setting; but, as we have seen, this does not necessitate an actual theological standpoint. On such levels it is perfectly possible to work without involving oneself in theological decisions, and even those who do make theological decisions do not, or should not, decide questions on these levels on theological grounds. But there are also other levels – let us call them the higher – where more theological questions are, if not quite inevitable, at least very natural. Yet the viability of proposals made on these higher levels never rests upon theological considerations alone, but rests on the data of the lower levels where it is subject to nontheological control. The existence of a lively dialogue between scripture and theology seems to me to depend on this sort of variability. In problems on these higher levels – and as an instance I would cite the question of the integration of scripture as a theological whole, the problem of how it can be understood to hang together as a meaningful totality – it is very natural, though not absolutely inevitable, that one should work with models of integration drawn from the past theological traditions of the church. But these models are not validated by the fact that they come out of that tradition: they are validated by the degree to which they make sense of the evidence that exists, evidence which has already been classified and to some degree interpreted on other levels of the total process of study.

Thus biblical study does exist as a recognizable discipline; it is neither necessarily separate from theology nor necessarily integrated with theology. If it is separate from theology, then there are certain things that it cannot properly do; it is thereby the poorer, and theology is the poorer too. But that loss cannot be made up by insisting that biblical study can only be theological. A little earlier I used the often-mentioned phrase 'the context of the church'. Theological study of the Bible does take place in the context of the church; but that is not the only context that it has. It also has a context in a wider academic community, and it can fully serve the context of the church only in so far as it respects also the integrity of modes of study and interpretation, valid within that community, over which theology as theology cannot pronounce. The social manifestation of this fact is the existence of the community of biblical scholarship, and this aspect of its character is perhaps more clearly manifest in the sphere of the Old Testament than in that of the New.

This lecture then is not calling for any revolutionary change in our practice: it is asking rather for understanding and acceptance of what we already have. This may not seem to be any very great achievement. But, Mr Vice-Chancellor, an inaugural lecture is after all a somewhat stylized occasion; and to have demonstrated that the actual is also possible may perhaps be felt to be a fitting theme for such a time.

3

Historical Reading and the Theological Interpretation of Scripture

The main purpose of this article is to enquire whether the historical reading of scripture – the 'historical-critical method' as it is often called – is ultimately a secular instrument which, while it may be of some use to theology, does not intrinsically belong to it, or whether it draws its legitimation from within the inner structure of Christian belief and therefore of valid theological thinking. The subject is a large one and I have no expectation of covering it within this limited space. In so far as I have any special contribution to offer, it consists in three things: First, some reference to recent writing on the subject; secondly, some fresh angles on the relation between history and faith; thirdly, some emphasis on the Old Testament, which I venture to hope will provide a picture slightly different from that which is found if we take the New Testament as point of departure.

It is said – and I do not guarantee the authenticity of the story – that Karl Barth was once asked about the historical-critical method. Barth – characteristically – appeared never to have heard of the expression. What was this? he asked. What could such a thing be? In what sense was it 'historical', and in what sense was it 'critical'? At the risk of being simple and naive, I will answer Barth's questions. 'Historical' reading of a text means a reading which aims at the reconstruction of spatial-temporal events in the past: it asks what was the actual sequence of the events to which the text refers, or what was the sequence of events by which the text came into existence. This constitutes the 'historical' component. Such historical reading is, I would further say, 'critical' in this sense, that it accepts the possibility that events were not in fact as they are described in the text: that things happened differently, or that the text was written at a different time, or by a different person. No operation is genuinely historical if it does not accept this critical component: in other words, being 'critical' is analytically involved in being historical.[1] It is therefore sufficient if we say simply 'historical reading': I would indeed prefer this to the customary term 'historical-critical method', which seems to suggest that some peculiar methodical procedure is involved. These observations are only preliminary and will be illustrated later in this lecture.

One of the commonest of all remarks is: 'Christianity is a historical religion.' As Professor Wiles has recently pointed out, it is by no means clear what this means.[2] What do people mean when they say this? Probably it is a general sentiment intended to support a wide variety of differing theological positions. It seems to break down into a general assertion plus a more particular assertion. The general assertion seems to be that Christianity, because it is a historical religion, is therefore a better religion than others which, it is implied, are not historical or are not historical in the same sense. Whether this general assertion is true or not can be left aside for the present. In fact, when this general assertion is made, it is usually supposed to form the basis for a more particular opinion, and, until this particular option is specified, it remains a largely empty claim. Thus, when people say that Christianity is a historical religion, they usually do this as part of an argument for their own preferred option within Christianity. At least six different options can easily be distinguished.

(1) For some it means that the historical course that Christianity has followed is thereby right and normative, that the tradition of the church, because it is a historical development, should therefore be accepted as inevitable and as valid. This is a traditional 'Catholic' option. (2) For others it means that, because the religion is a historical one, its documents must be subject to the same kind of historical scrutiny as the documents of any other movement or ideology. This might be called an academic historical and often secular option. (3) For others again it means that, since the religion is a historical one, therefore the historical assertions made in its documents must be considered as historically accurate or at least very largely so. This is a familiar conservative biblicist or fundamentalist option. (4) Others again use our remark to validate a particular way of thinking:

according to this option, Christian thinking does not work with a timeless logic but with categories of past and future, and if you are to understand this faith you have to think within a historically-controlled system of thought. This option has been familiar in the biblical theology of the post-war period. (5) Others again think that, since the true historicity of human life lies not in the past but in orientation to the world in which we exist, even the past being understood through, and as a part of, our self-awareness of life and the world, the stress in Christianity must be upon its impact upon 'me' in my present situation. This is a familiar existentialist approach. (6) Others understand it to mean that, since Christianity is a historical religion, the religion should be made to rest upon that limited element in the sources which can stand as historically probable or reliable. This is a familiar position of the older liberal Protestantism.

This gives us already half a dozen options, and combinations between these are possible, indeed are quite common. But this means that the common claim that Christianity is a historical religion is a very vague blanket assertion, for it does not in itself specify what sort of relation between religion and history is meant. Thus, far from providing authority for any one or more of the specific options, it itself becomes meaningful only when it receives its content from one of them.

Now part of the basis for most or all of these options is the narrative literary form of the Bible itself: not all of it, but much of it, tells a story specifying events in the past. When people say that Christian faith has a deep rootage or foundation in history, they are commonly thinking of these events, and specifically of events which not only happened but which also are soteriologically essential, in the sense that if these events had not happened the faith would be vain. The crucifixion and resurrection of Jesus Christ is of course the central example: Christian thinkers and theologians, contrary to the impression they sometimes give, are rather well agreed about this.

Now before we go further we should note one of the main reasons why all this has been important in the history of Christian thought. Certainly Christian faith and doctrine has always in all ages had its anchorage in the historical, in the sense just defined, namely that the essential saving events had taken place in the past and that essential written sources told of these events and of the sayings, rules, laws and so on which were communicated along with them. But though this anchorage in the past was always *there*, it is only in relatively modern times that people have begun to say that this historical character of Christianity was *the main* essential of it. During much of the history of Christianity, and this is true of Judaism also, the faith has been presented and understood in a different way. It has been understood as a great system of beliefs and relations – people at one time spoke of 'the Christian system' – all of which had basically been true at all times, with only limited qualifications which in any case were absorbed within the system. The system allowed for a certain amount of change and historical growth: for instance, it was believed that some of the laws of the Old Testament, while valid in ancient times, had ceased to be fully applicable. Change of this kind was specified and accepted within the system itself. Once this limited amount of change had been allowed for, the system was a great corpus of truths and beliefs that had always been true and always would be true. Contrary to general opinion, the fact that there were strong historical beliefs, such as the beliefs in the events of the life, death and resurrection of Jesus, did not contradict the fact that Christianity as a whole worked as a relatively static system, for that static system incorporated the historical affirmations within it. The system covered everything: the Trinity, the incarnation, the nature of heaven and hell, the meaning of baptism, the number of orders in the ministry, the relations between church and state, the keeping of Sunday, the colour of vestments worn by the clergy, and the question whether you knelt to pray or stood up or just sat. And this way of looking at Christianity has been quite strong until recently, and some of our outlooks on the faith are still derived from it. Moreover, as I shall suggest, there were reasons as far back as the Bible itself why it came to be so. But it is in reaction against this 'system' view of Christianity that so many people of dynamism have insisted that faith rests upon events in history, and not upon conformity to a great static system. It is this powerful liberating influence more than anything else that has led so many to insist on historical events as the essential milieu of revelation.

We go back therefore to the function of past events. It is important to observe that this soteriological function of events cannot be extrapolated to cover all events mentioned in scripture. When people say that Christianity is dependent on historical events, in the sense that but for these events the faith would be vain, the number of events that they have in mind is quite small; and this is the difference between scripture and creeds. The passion and resurrection of Jesus Christ is the main specific historical reference in the creeds. Scripture on the other hand mentions large numbers of historical or apparently historical events, but no one supposes that all of these bear a relation to Christianity analogical to Jesus' crucifixion under Pontius Pilate or his resurrection from the dead. Christian salvation does not depend in this way on the event that in the thirty-eighth year of Asa king of Judah Ahab the son of Omri began to reign over Israel (I Kings 16.29) or that in Ahab's days Hiel of Bethel rebuilt the city of Jericho (v. 34). Similarly, in the New Testament story itself, no one supposes that there would have been no Christian salvation, and thus no ground for Christian faith, if Jesus had not in fact wept in the garden of Gethsemane, or if the prophet Agabus did not in fact foretell a great famine (Acts 11.28), or if that famine did not indeed take place in the days of Claudius. Thus the number of the historical events upon which the faith is intrinsically dependent, in the sense that the faith would be false and our salvation vain if these events did not happen, is exceedingly small; and the argument from soteriological necessity does not give a theological grounding for the reliability of scriptural reports of events, except for very few cases.

This is granted even by very conservative opinion, though the force of the argument is commonly not realized. Ultra-conservative opinions may be shocked if one says that Jesus did not really change the water into wine, or if one says that Hiel did not really rebuild Jericho in Ahab's time, but this is a matter of assurance and implication, not of intrinsic functional importance for salvation. Ultra-conservatives will worry about Hiel's rebuilding of Jericho because they reason thus: if the Bible is not accurate in saying this about Hiel, how can we know that it is accurate in telling about the crucifixion and resurrection of Jesus Christ, or indeed about anything else? But even the most ultra of conservatives does not suppose that the gospel would be falsified and the faith rendered vain if Hiel had not rebuilt Jericho. Thus there is a wide gap between the actual narrative form and detailed content of the Bible and the ground that can be covered by any argument from the soteriological function of events.

With this we can pass on to another aspect. When we say that Christianity is a historical religion, we may mean – and here again most of us are agreed in this – that its contact with God takes place within the historical milieu, the changing scene of human life along the line of past and future. But Christianity is related to this milieu not only along the line of the arrow that points towards the past but also along the line of the arrow that points towards the future. In this respect an enormous difference has been made by the future-directed theologies of our time. Christianity is an eschatological religion, and that is just as important as to say that it is a historical religion. History and eschatology lie on the same plane and work in the same milieu, but though it is the same milieu it cannot have the same implications. Historical research into the future is not a practical possibility, and even in these bad days futurology has not yet become a recognized academic discipline. A whole series of problems that arise for theology from its rootage in past history do not arise from its rootage in future history or eschatology: in particular of course the whole historical-critical question. If we think of Christianity as equally poised between past history and future history, and in that sense a historical religion, there is a strong disparity between the two, in that historical method, as a mode of investigation of sources, falls heavily upon the past component but scarcely at all upon the future component. It was the misfortune of the church that, at the same time as the past component came under difficulties from historical criticism, the church itself was more and more assuming and asserting that the past component was the essential one, and this has continued to be so until very recent times indeed.

Now this is of very great importance for the doctrine of scripture. The dominant view of scripture in modern times has made it dependent on *antecedent* revelation. *In the past* revelation took place, and biblical narratives report this revelation, or witness to it, or interpret it: in any case, the revelation precedes the scripture, just as it precedes the church. But it is possible to give a quite different account of the implication of scripture in revelation. If one starts from the Old Testament and its involvement in Christian salvation, one is forced to do so. Jesus Christ came into a world where there was already a people of God and already a scripture. The scripture, and the people of God with its then tradition and its inner crises, provided the conceptuality within which the coming of Jesus was intelligible. To say this is not to deny that there was also antecedent revelation. But the essential function of scripture was to lend intelligibility to events

that were to come. Its basic soteriological direction was towards
the future.

When this is perceived, it enables us to deal with much of
the narrative material of the Bible in a different way. Narratives
are not necessarily written because of a primary interest in the
past. They can be written for a quite different reason: they can
be written to provide pictures of the promises of God which
will come to pass in the future. Even if their literal purport
concerns the past, their theological function and purpose may
be directed towards the future.

Quite a lot of the Old Testament narrative material can be
seen in this way. The author of Genesis did not tell the story of
Abraham telling his wife Sarah (twice in succession, followed
by the same story about Isaac also) that she should give herself
out to be his sister in order to keep him out of danger, because
he was interested in the historical Abraham. Perhaps the story
– and the other Abraham stories, or parts of them – were told
not because the writer was interested in faithfully recording
how things were back in the second millennium, but because
he was interested in the fulfilment of the future promise of God
which was still to come. The same is true of the chronological
system of the Old Testament, which marks the numbers of
years from the creation of the world, probably because it looks
for the coming of some eschaton which will be intelligible in
relation to these figures. The books of Kings end with the
information about how Jehoiachin, in the thirty-seventh year of
his exile, was restored to favour by Amel-Marduk king of Babylon, not because it was an important event in the past history
of the Israelite kingdoms, but because it was a sign pointing
towards the possible future restoration of the Davidic dynasty.
In general, for much of the Old Testament material, even when
past events are being narrated this is not necessarily out of an
interest in past history but because of patterns of future hope.
Thus one of the great traditional terms applied to scripture is
misleading. It is wrong to think of scripture as a 'record': it is
not in essence a record, though in places it may incidentally be
so. Even in its past narratives its function is often not to be a
record of past events but to present paradigms for thinking
about the present or hoping for the future. And the same would
apply to many important areas of the New Testament also.

The narrative materials of the Old Testament (and of the
New) should be classed not as history, but at the most as

'history-like' (Hans Frei's expression[3]). The material was not in essence history, it was story that included substantial historical elements. The writers were not historians, they were story-tellers whose stories included much historical material.

That whole set of ideas upon which post-war biblical theology built so much was in fact the greatest weakness of that movement. Israel's genius was never directed towards the interpretation of history, which would have had to mean that she continued to interpret history in the same manner, as history went on. It was directed rather to the telling of a story, a very long but finite story. The story was not simply history: on the one hand it included legendary elements, on the other its motivation was often not really in the past at all but in the present and future.

The story was a sort of foundation story: beginning from the creation of the world, it ran down to the establishment of some kind of normative situation or the completion of some all-important stage. When this point was reached the story largely stopped. During the Persian empire, when very important developments in the Jewish community and its religious structure took place, there was no attempt to recount the mighty acts of God in these events. Short and episodic narratives like the material of Ezra, Nehemiah and Esther do not aspire to the *heilsgeschichtlich* scope and depth of the older stories. Far from it being extremely difficult for the Jewish mind to pass over to a non-historical mode of perception of the world, it was extremely easy, and has remained so. In Hellenistic times, far from it being true that a historical apperception was peculiar to Israel, it was mainly where it was in contact with Greek thinking and Greek society that Judaism was productive in historiography. There are many sorts of literature at Qumran, but history is not a genre represented there. In fact a historical mode of perception was never a primary mark of distinction between Israel and her neighbours: on the contrary, as Albrektson has shown,[4] it was a common element shared with the ancient Near East. Moreover, it was a common element shared also with the Graeco-Roman world. Virgil's *Aeneid* was a theological legitimation, in story form, of the Augustan principate, and Livy's history of Rome was a depiction of the will of the gods expressed in history towards the Roman people. And Greek culture had its foundation story just as Hebrew culture had: the Homeric poems were a story about particular individuals, set

in a specific historical context (and one not very remote from
that of the earlier mighty acts of God towards Israel!), interact-
ing with the gods, who intervene on the scene of history.

There is no need to exaggerate the similarities, for the differences are enormous. It remains true that the existence of a basic
foundation story is a common point and not a matter of distinctiveness. The idea that the Hebrew perception of reality was
fundamentally historical, while that of the Graeco-Roman world
was radically unhistorical, will not stand up to examination.
Finally, this means that the move of both Judaism, and later
Christianity, from something mediated through historical
events into a great system of beliefs and relations, basically true
at all times with only limited qualifications, was not nearly as
difficult as it has seemed. Both in the Old Testament and in the
New we can see in some of the later sources a tendency to
harden the living faith into a system of just this kind. And thus,
great as is the difference between Greek philosophy and Jewish-
Christian faith, it is a mere matter of fact that no mode of
thinking has shown itself to be so easily combinable with Christianity as Greek philosophy; and none has exercised so great an
influence upon it, up to the present day.

Now the essential thing in this is that biblical narrative
belongs to literary form: that is to say, the fact that texts are
narrative does not in itself demonstrate that the perception lying
behind them is a historical one, interested in correct reports
about the past or the true reconstruction of it. If I understand
rightly the profound but difficult book of Hans Frei, the crisis
of biblical interpretation came when historical reference began
to be taken to be the major and central issue in the validity of
scripture.

> When the pattern of meaning is no longer firmly ingredient in the
> story and the occurrence character of the text but becomes a function
> of a quasi-independent interpretative stance, literal and figural read-
> ing draw apart.[5]

According to Frei, and if I understand him rightly I also agree
with him, biblical narrative is a consequent and coherent story,
in which historical reference is an *element* of the sense *within the
story*.[6] But when the church met the first modern questionings
of these narratives and of their historical validity, it responded
apologetically by insisting that the historical reference was true
and that this was the essential basis of Christianity. In this

conce the insistence on 'what really happened', which conservatives used against Deists and other doubters, was itself also at the origin of the historical-critical questioning.

The first impact of historical reading was not on the Protestant understanding of scripture but upon the Roman Catholic view of the tradition. It was anti-traditional: it affected not scripture but extra-biblical documents and traditions. Three examples may be mentioned. In the fifteenth century various persons, and notably Lorenzo Valla (to whom I must add Reginald Pecock, Fellow of Oriel College and later Bishop of Chichester)[7], showed that the Donation of Constantine was a forgery: historically there had been no such donation, and, as for the document, it came from a later time and was a fabrication. In 1624 Ludwig Cappellus showed, against the tradition that the vowel points of the Hebrew Bible had been given to Moses on Mount Sinai, that these points had been added only after the fifth or sixth century AD. In 1684 Humphrey Hody, Fellow of Wadham College, in his *Contra historiam Aristeae de LXX interpretibus dissertatio*, demonstrated that the so-called Letter of Aristeas, in which the origins of the Greek Old Testament are set forth, was not written by that person and that the Septuagint originated in a quite different manner. Historical study of this sort showed that the great system of beliefs, as it existed, had not always existed: the late medieval scheme of the Papacy, the Decretals and so on had not existed in the Fathers, much less in the New Testament. The effect of this critical operation was to create a layering, a sort of stratificational separation, in the picture of the past.

From the later eighteenth century onwards, the same sort of stratification began to be carried out in the study of the Bible, and here it was Protestantism in the first place that was affected. Though it had been supposed that Moses had written the Pentateuch, it was now said that it had been written in many stages and that what was said in the later stages was different from what had been asserted in the earlier. Thus one main effect of historical study was to break down the conception of the religion as one great system of truths and beliefs, more or less perpetually so existing, and introduce essential distinctions between successive layers of material. In this sense historical reading has an important positive role in enabling the text itself to be heard as against the theological tradition which has customarily interpreted it.

Now when a mode of reading, seeking to identify and reconstruct the historical referent, was applied to biblical materials,
it was not difficult to see that what had happened was in some
cases very different from what the biblical text, if evaluated as
an historical record, had said. Sophisticated modern theologians
sometimes smile at the naive concept of 'what really happened'
and point to the great methodological difficulties involved in
saying what happened, and how great are the differences
between good historians themselves in doing this, even in giving an account of (say) Napoleon, without having transfigura-
tions and resurrections to cope with into the bargain. But these
sophisticated calculations overlook the rather simple and gross
character of the differences as they appeared to the earlier students of the Bible, whether they were sceptical or credulous.
Take the story of the exodus and the march of the Israelites
from Egypt to Canaan. According to a major biblical source, the
Israelites were at this time a large and united people of twelve
tribes: there were over 600,000 males of military age (603,550
according to Num. 1.46), plus enough women, children and
aged to make up perhaps two million. They marched in a clearly
defined order, camping nightly in a formation of square design,
each tribe in its defined place. They entered Canaan as a unitary
military force under Joshua and fought a series of successful
campaigns.

As against this picture modern scholars, influenced by
counter-indications in other parts of the biblical text, plus non-
biblical and archaeological evidences, have worked out a quite
different picture of what took place. There are of course a variety
of opinions; but according to one influential line of thinking,
which I take as an example, there was no united nation of Israel
at this time. No doubt some group had an escape from Egypt
which they regarded as miraculous, but this was only a small
group, perhaps only a couple of hundred people. Far from the
nation marching to Canaan as a great united army in prescribed
order, there may have been no more than several smallish
groups who got into Canaan by different routes. Some of the
people whose descendants later counted as Israel had probably
never gone to Egypt and had never been out of Canaan. Still
more, some allege, it was not an army of incoming Israelites
that took over the land, but disaffected groups from within the
society. If this is so, then the picture drawn in the Pentateuchal
sources is a legendary construction from later times. It makes

no difference to my argument whether these interpretations are right. What it means is that, if some element of these reconstructions is right, even if only a small element, then there is a very gross disparity between the surface account of the biblical sources, if they are taken as a historical record, and the events as they really happened. No doubt 'what really happened' is a very inadequate concept for the modern philosophy of history; but for instances like this it is quite adequate, because the differences in question are gross. Now this exemplifies for us the difference between story and history. The biblical narrative account is of the greatest importance, but it belongs to story, to literary form, it is the story as told in the text, whether true or not, fiction or fact, reliable or unreliable, legend, myth or history. History is about what really happened. It may not be able to tell us precisely, definitively or incontrovertibly what really happened; but what really happened is the assumed standard by which it operates.

The reader might however be inclined to say: forget about the numbers of the children of Israel, let's get on to something that is important, like the miracles of Jesus or the resurrection. And I understand the feeling. But that is what cannot be done if one is to understand how the historical reading of scripture grew. This is one reason why the Old Testament is so important and why it can lead to a better understanding than the New Testament, so often bogged down in its questions about the Jesus of history. The marginal cases, like the number of the Israelites on their march, are very important. In these apparently marginal cases hundreds of decisions are taken which suggest that events happened in a way substantially different from the way in which the Bible – if taken as a historical report – describes them. The larger the number of these marginal decisions, the more difficult it becomes to say that the story of Jesus is exempted from the same sort of decision. The more one admits that, with the numbers of the Israelites on their march, or with the dates and genealogies of the Pentateuch, or with this or that 'marginal' discrepancy in the New Testament itself, there may be an alternative explanation and things did not happen exactly as they stand in the text, the more docetic does it become to take certain more 'central' incidents in the story of Jesus and say that that sort of explanation is not permitted here. The marginal cases within scripture, plus the host of comparable cases in extra-scriptural documents, crowd in upon the cases that seem to be essential, demanding a reason why they should have different treatment. From this point of view it is clear that the full fundamentalist position, namely that *all* these narratives must be completely right, is a very rational response.

Now I have already suggested ways in which the historical reading of scripture is not merely a secular alternative to theological interpretation but depends on properly theological functions. Firstly, it serves as an important means by which we may distinguish the actual meaning of scripture from that which has been traditionally assumed; or, conversely, opposition to historical criticism comes characteristically from currents which support the maintenance and dominion of a particular *tradition* – conservative evangelicalism and fundamentalism are an obvious example. Secondly, as scholars like Ebeling and Stuhlmacher have argued,[8] it has an anti-docetic function which keeps biblical interpretation closer to reality. In general it has very substantial achievements to its credit, and this not simply in the specifically historical function of telling what happened (on this side we remain rather uncertain) but in the more specifically theological function of interpreting scripture theologically. For it is safe to say that, throughout that side of scholarship which has sought to interpret the Bible theologically, the achievements of scholars whose work has been fertilized by ˙ historical and critical reading have enormously outweighed those of scholars who have opposed that mode of reading and its results.

Nevertheless there remain very considerable doubts about the historical approach to scripture and these have to be looked at carefully.[9] I will put it in two ways. First of all, though I have already suggested ways in which historical reading may have a positively theological function, and will hope to add more, few of us, or none of us, today think that it is in itself a directly theological operation which will itself uncover the inner revelation within scripture. Of the various options with which I began, only one, the sixth, the older liberal Protestantism, can be said to have contained currents which thought in this way. According to one characteristic liberal approach, historical study would strip off the later dogmatic accretions and mythological miracle-elements and what would be left would be the basic revelatory material, the historical Jesus and the like. Practically no scholars at work today think in this way. That whole aspect of the liberal approach has as a matter of fact almost completely disappeared. If the modern scholar wants to read the Bible historically it is not because he is in principle sceptical of dogma, of miracles, of the resurrection and the like. People do not reason that miracles and resurrections are *a priori* impossible, so that a different interpretation of the texts narrating them must be found; they reason rather that, though these things are with God entirely possible, it is doubtful if they provide appropriate explanations of the literary and historical questions. All of this is markedly different from the traditional liberal approach to scripture. 'Critical historical theology is not identical with liberal theology':[10] one might go further, and say that it is markedly different from liberal theology. What is striking is how much of the analysis and elucidation achieved in the liberal period survives and continues to be valuable and indeed basic in our modern situation.

There is however one aspect remaining that seems to me to be a survival from the older liberal organization of biblical study, and I refer to the genre of literature known as *Introductions* to the Old or New Testament, *Einleitungswissenschaft* as it is known in German. If you read a book called an 'introduction' to the Old Testament, what do you find? You find the results of a careful and detailed literary-historical analysis of the books of the Old Testament. Now there is nothing wrong with this except its name, and the concept that lies behind the name. The contents of such books are excellent, but they are not in fact introduction, initiation; they are *results*. What the reader finds in an *Introduction* is the results of many years of painstaking analysis of the biblical books. In German terms, these works are not *Einleitung* but *Endergebnis*. Why then were they called *Introductions*? Because in the liberal period it was thought that this sort of thing was the essential mode of entry into the literature, the results of which would enable the reader to be clear in his mind what was reliable material and what was not. In other words, historical and literary-critical analysis was the direct introduction, the gateway, to theological appreciation. Now pedagogically speaking this has been damaging to our subject. Why? Except for those few who retain the essentials of the old liberal approach, historical criticism is not an introduction which by its own logic leads on to theological appreciation; rather, it is a different and separate operation which puts the same material through a different hermeneutical process. Starting from the biblical texts, you can go through two interpretative processes, and one may do them both at the same time, but one of them leads out into literary and historical results and the other into theological evaluation. But if you teach the former as the essential 'introduction' to the subject, the beginning student is almost inevitably given the impression that he is being forced to embark upon a secularizing and de-theologizing process; and this is one of the deeper reasons why there is a strong reaction against the whole critical approach. This is only made worse by the fact that introduction, so conceived, seeming to be a more objective and clearly defined subject, is more easily examined and comes to have an even larger place in the total scheme of biblical study. In all this I do not say one word against the content of our excellent introductions to the Old and New Testament, except perhaps that there seem to be too many of them; but the average student should assimilate these not as the beginning stage but as a final stage in his process of biblical study. To put it in the converse way, the education of students in biblical materials should *begin* with theological evaluation and this should proceed *pari passu* with historical and literary introduction. I believe that this would do much to overcome the disillusionment occasioned by our contemporary educational praxis and to reduce the consequent flight into anti-critical positions.

This is strengthened by an important methodological factor: though, if I am right, literary-critical analysis and theological evaluation go in opposite directions and reach different sets of results, they have important common elements in their working. Literary and historical analysis is not a merely inductive discipline working from disparate objective data: it depends on the trying out of constructive hypotheses about the theological position of (say) the P source, the Deuteronomist, the mind of St Paul, whatever it may be. Such proposed assessments do not, indeed, constitute theology in the full sense of the word, but they constitute a sort of pre-theology, a preliminary assessment of what may be there in the material; and such a preliminary assessment is not derived purely inductively from the text, it is in considerable degree an imaginative construct which is then set against the data in order to see if it works. Correspondingly, theological evaluation is not something that can proceed separately and independently of literary and historical factors. Thus, as I conceive it, though the two processes are going in different directions and leading towards different sets of results, they also have an important common area. The student's task is not to complete one of these before attempting the other, but rather to work on scripture itself with the realization that his operations go in more than one direction at the same time. Thus, to sum up, historical reading and theological evaluation are so related that neither can be properly carried out under the impression that the other does not exist or does not matter. Historical reading does not provide, and should not provide, the basis or logical foundation upon which theological evaluation must be built; but no useful theological evaluation can be carried out if it denies, evades or obviates the fact that this other direction of interpretation is also being validly carried out.

In a sense, however, the most important way in which historical reading has operated is not, as people suppose, its direct influence upon beliefs about what happened or who wrote this book or that and when. This, enormous as it seems at first sight, is less serious in the end than another factor: historical reading has gained control of the *semantic* linkages within the text and its language. This is the deepest-lying shift of emphasis. It is deeper-lying because it goes back to a time before the rise of many critical questions properly so-called, to before there were questions about sources in the Pentateuch or about the historical reliability of the Fourth Gospel; it goes back to questions about the literal and the grammatical sense of which the middle ages, in Judaism as well as in Christianity, were aware, and which came to expression also in the Reformation. It seems to me thus to be deep-lying and also to be irreversible. It is on this side that the dominion of historical reading is most complete; those who most resist its historical consequences have themselves accepted its dominion in this respect.

Yet exactly here there is room for the historical reading of scripture to improve. Too often it has been allowed to become a harshly limited concentration on a narrow band of meaning understood to be the 'original', and it has thus tended to reduce to one, and that a very narrow one, the variety of layers of meaning to be seen in a multi-faceted literature like the Bible. Against this in recent years a number of voices have been raised: I think of a variety of interpretative directions loosely associated under the name structuralism, and also of the position pioneered by Brevard Childs, with its emphasis on the final canonical form of the text, as against the traditional critical emphasis on the 'original' meaning. We may take as example a recent argument put forward by Childs concerning Deutero-Isaiah.[11] He fully accepts the normal critical explanation of this material, which places it in the mid-sixth century, long after the original Isaiah. But the present context, while historically secondary, 'is a highly reflective, intentional setting which was considered so important that the original sixth-century context was almost totally obliterated by those who transmitted the material'. Again,

> Even though the message of Second Isaiah was once addressed to real people in a particular historical situation, the canonical shape of these chapters has drained them of their historical particularity and has subordinated the original message to a new role within the canon.

The effect of this is that the message of Second Isaiah becomes a 'prophetic word not tied to a specific historical referent, but directed to the future'. Similarly, elsewhere: 'the shaping process [within the formation of the canonical book] altered the semantic level on which a passage originally functioned by assigning it a less-than-literal role within the canonical context'; and the juxtaposition of materials from different sources may have the effect of assigning to a passage 'a degree of figurative interpretation once-removed from the literal sense of the original language'.[12] These and similar arguments are very significant; they show up a defect in the critical approach as it has generally been practised and, by opening a window towards the figurative sense, they are creative – as Childs himself intends – in opening a window also towards the traditional exegesis of the church.

Obviously there are important things to be heard here. Does it mean however that an essentially historical reading should be abandoned and replaced by some other, or is Childs' proposal rather perhaps a correction and improvement of historical reading itself? I am inclined to think that it is the latter. The whole earlier historical movement, as it worked in spheres like ancient literature and religion, and notably in a subject like Hebrew philology, was mistakenly biased towards *origins*: things were explained if you knew what their origins were, and the origins were more important than the results. As we see it today, historical reading should move more towards an understanding of *effects* rather than an emphasis on *origins*. Processes like redaction criticism have already begun to move us in this direction.

Can one however hope to go still further and restore a mode of reading that would not seek to be historical at all, that would look only at the forms and patterns of the text, without asking any questions either about dates or historical events or about sources and authorships? The text would then have its meaning in itself, and not in events or activities lying behind it and extraneous to it. This is one way in which a structuralist principle might be expressed. About this I can offer only the following brief remarks. First, such a non-historical reading could be salutary in some ways and could lead to important results for certain sorts of literature. Secondly, however, if it was accompanied by a complete or deliberate ignoring of the historical reading it would almost certainly have severely negative effects. This is because, thirdly, we are now deeply imbued with the belief that the sense of biblical passages, or of most of them, lies in the external events to which they refer, so that readers using this method would almost certainly assume the literal historicity of all events mentioned, thus destroying the very method just set up. Fourthly, the theological effects of such a mode of reading would be limited or even damaging: great as is the trouble caused us by the modern belief that the meaning of scripture lies in the events it describes, that belief is grounded, even if only partially, in the realities of the Christian faith. Salvation belongs not to the networks of meaning within a text, not even the text of the Bible, but to a set of people and events. In other words, it is not probable that we can get out of our dilemmas by opting for any mode of reading which would systematically bypass the historical questions. Even if the Bible as a book could be studied in a non-referential way, paying no attention to anything outside the text itself, the structure of Christian faith does not work in that way; and if it did so, our faith would become a faith in *a book* to an extent hitherto scarcely dreamed of even in the most biblicist sort of circles. Nevertheless it is quite possible that such a reading might be added to, or used as supplement to, an evaluation that looks for the historical events mentioned in the narrative. Possibly some parts of scripture would be read for historical reference while others were not: few, after all, have read the book of Job for its historical reference, nor has anyone of sense read the parables in that way, asking, shall we say, for the date of the Good Samaritan or the cultural background of the Prodigal Son.

It is now time to conclude all this by considering its consequences for our systematic doctrinal conceptions, as they bear upon the doctrine of scripture itself. What seems to follow, if these considerations are to be accommodated in our doctrinal thinking, is not so much an alteration in the *content* of the doctrine of scripture as an alteration in its *positioning*. We have long been accustomed to a positioning of the doctrine of scripture which makes it follow the doctrine of revelation. The order can be set out diagrammatically as: God → revelation → scripture. In suggesting a reordering of this scheme I follow in part the ideas of David Kelsey in his significant book *The Uses of Scripture in Recent Theology*, notably in his final chapter.[13] Scripture should be doctrinally positioned under the doctrine of the church. Thus we would have the order God → church → tradition → scripture. Scripture follows tradition as a special case within the totality of tradition, and Christian tradition factually and historically defines itself as a sort of tradition which has within itself a particular express written segment defined and accepted canonically. Revelation has no one unique point of attachment in relation to this scheme, but different aspects of what has traditionally been lumped together under revelation would attach to various points. For example, one can still talk of revelation in space and time events antecedent to scripture, but one can with equal validity talk of revelation coming out of the impact of scripture in the context of the church, of revelation as a future event to which scripture points, and so on.

Within such a model, where would the legitimation of the historical and critical reading of scripture be found? Is it in the last resort a secular method which may be helpful to theological understanding but does not intrinsically belong to it? Or does it have a truly theological legitimation? Ebeling in his well-known essay, cited above, ties historical-critical reading to the Protestant principle of justification by faith. He points to the way in which the growth of historical awareness was linked with the Reformation movement and insists that 'the critical historical method has essentially a deep inner connexion with the Reformers' doctrine of justification'. In Ebeling's judgment it is essential that 'encounter with the historic revelation takes place solely in hearing the Word', and this means that there must be absolutely no means of human security, ontological, sacramental or hierarchical. Among these means of human security Ebeling counts also that sort of clinging to the historical reliability of scriptural narratives that goes along with any rejection of historical and critical reading.

> The shattering of all historical assurances that supposedly render the decision of faith superfluous is completely in line with the struggle against the saving significance of good works. . . . The *sola fide* destroys all secretly docetic views of revelation which evade the historicalness of revelation by making it a history *sui generis*, a sacred area from which the critical historical method must be anxiously debarred.

Thus, to sum up, those who adopted the critical approach were – in spite of their mistakes and the paradox of their position – really reasserting the fundamental principle of the Reformers in the intellectual situation of the modern age. Conversely, it must be questioned 'whether a theology which evades the claims of the critical historical method still has any idea at all of the genuine meaning of the Reformers' doctrine of justification', however much such a theology reiterates the formulae of justification by faith.[14]

This is a powerful argument and very well worked out by Ebeling; and as a negative argument it seems to be very right. Historically it seems true that the critical reading of scripture has an essential connection with Protestantism and justification by faith. It is equally certain that those who deny historical criticism fall into a docetic position and abandon the centrality of faith exactly as Ebeling says. On the positive side, however, one may doubt whether this argument provides a sufficient *positive* basis for historical and critical reading. The argument is predicated upon a cleft between Protestant and Catholic theology much more deep and final than many of us could accept. (This is true also of the more recent formulation of the question by Stuhlmacher.) And there is, perhaps, a legitimate conservative counter-argument which would say: justification by faith is just not about this sort of thing. It is concerned with the problem of salvation through works of the law, and it is not concerned with the assurance of accuracy in historical reports within scripture, so that it cannot legitimately be applied to that problem. And, while that objection can no doubt be countered, so that Ebeling's analogy with the question of justification by faith can be made to hold, it still does not seem to form a sufficient basis for a positive grounding of historical and critical reading.

Much as I sympathize with the spirit of Ebeling's argumentation in general, my own proposals would go in another direction. I would suggest that the true legitimation of historical and critical reading lies in the relation between scripture, tradition and the church. Tradition is not an unchanging metaphysical entity but is something that we know rightly only if we know it historically: as we all know, we cannot read back the doctrinal positions of the nineteenth century into the sixteenth or into the fourth. No one can read the Athanasian Creed as if it existed in the time of St Paul. The tradition has to be seen in many historical layers. We can do this only because we read the documents historically: historical reading reveals that there are many different layers in the tradition. Now the effect of historical reading upon scripture is to make scripture in this respect more like tradition than it at first appeared to be. In patristics and in later doctrinal history historical reading was always easier: the different layers of the tradition were naturally preserved more separate from one another. What Irenaeus wrote was to be found in a different book from what Athanasius wrote, and that was in a different book from what St Thomas Aquinas wrote. But in scripture this was not so. The effect of scripture was to foreshorten the tradition, within the biblical period, to an astonishing degree. Precisely because it became scripture, and because practically no extra-scriptural tradition from the biblical period survived, scripture if read just as it stands conceals much or most of the development of tradition that has gone into its own making. The effect of the historical reading of scripture was not that we got closer to the centre of revelation but – as we now see it – that scripture was re-expanded into a far greater number of dimensions. It has thus worked to restore to scripture the same sort of status that we apply automatically to the history and tradition of the church.

If this is so, and if we use for the conception of scripture the sort of model which I have just outlined, then historical reading, without claiming to be the sole possible mode of reading, has actually increased the possibility of our understanding scripture in its proper theological function. The entire depth of layering that we now discern through redaction criticism and other such processes would never have been seen if we had not embarked upon historical reading of scripture. As for authority, it remains an uncertain question whether the authority of scripture means the authority of the books themselves or the authority of the people from whom these books came. On the model I have put before you it is not necessary to make the choice: the authority can lie in both. It lies in the people – ancient Israel and the earliest church – from whom these texts came, in their life and their history; but also, functioning in another way, it lies in the text they developed out of their own tradition and eventually left to us as their official written communication. But if we had not embarked upon historical reading most of these people, and their work, would never have been known to us.

4

Has the Bible any Authority?

Well, we are faced with the question, 'Has the Bible any authority?', and I will begin straight away by answering with a vigorous 'Yes'. The question for me is not in the first place *whether* the Bible has authority or not, but why it has authority and how, in what measure and for what purposes and in what relations. So let us begin with what seems the most basic of these questions, '*Why* does the Bible have any authority, or why should it have any authority?' The answer is, I think, as follows: the Bible has authority because its authority, in some form or other, is built into the structure of Christian faith and the Christian religion. Being a Christian means – among other things – being tied up with the God of the Bible, with biblical ideas of God and traditions about him, with Jesus Christ, about whom almost our only source of guidance lies in the Bible as primary written source. In Kantian terms, involvement with the Bible is analytic in being a Christian: you can't first become a Christian and then consider whether, as an optional extra, synthetically in Kant's term, some sort of involvement with the Bible might be added on. Being a Christian is not simply being a theist, believing that there is a deity; it is believing in a particular God, the God who has manifested himself in a way that has some sort of unique and specific expression in the Bible. I now want to expand these insights in several directions.

First of all, I don't want to overstress the last point that I have made, as if to suggest that there is no connection at all between Christian faith and philosophical theism, as if to say that you have either a philosophical religion or a biblical religion but you can't have both, you have to choose absolutely between the two. That may be so, and some people have considered it so;

but then some people take the opposite side, and feel that
biblical faith has to be structured and even perhaps corrected
through philosophical insights which are not of actual biblical
origin. As far as I am concerned today, I do not have to take a
side in that ancient dispute. Let it be granted that something
valuable may be known of God through human reasoning and
human experience, apart from the Bible. Let it be agreed even
that some such philosophical framework may be necessary if
we are to make the truths of the Bible accessible and meaningful
in our own experience. I am not sure that I myself assert these
things, but let us grant them. Even granting the maximum
possible scope to the significance of philosophical theism or to
human moral sense or human experience as a source of the
knowledge of God, it remains true, I believe, that the God of
Christians is in essence the God of Abraham, of Isaac and of
Jacob, and not the God of the philosophers, as Pascal, himself
no mean philosophical thinker, put it. What may be known of
God philosophically is not enough to provide the basis for a
church: it does not provide the richness, the colour, the detail,
the history, the personalities, the words and speeches, the
incidents. It is this enormous variety that supports the liturgy
and the preaching of the churches and makes a church into
what it is.

Secondly, the Bible is involved in all this not as a true book
which contains true information about God and about various
other persons and past events. The Bible is more a battleground
than a book of true facts. Holy Scripture has a function in the
winning of salvation. We can illustrate this well from the role
of the Old Testament in the life and teaching of Jesus himself.
In his time there was already a scripture, and there was also a
religious tradition that sought to interpret that scripture. Jesus'
dialogue with Jewish leaders probed into the area of problems
that lay between the scripture and its alleged interpretation
within the people of God; and, as the gospels depict it, it was
this probing that led to the rejection of Jesus, his trial and
crucifixion – all in very complicated, and historically difficult,
ways. But it was the existence of a holy scripture, already recognized, that provided the intellectual basis upon which salvation
was achieved. Scripture thus has a soteriological function.
Equally, scripture provided for Jesus himself the intellectual
framework within which he conceptualized his own mission
and message. Scripture is fundamental to the church of God,

not because it is a book of true facts about God and about past events, but because it is built into the way in which salvation itself was achieved.

Thirdly, this means that our involvement with the Bible is part of our general religious involvement with God, with the church, and with salvation. The authority of the Bible is one part of the complex of problems that are addressed by Christian faith. Our acceptance of the authority of the Bible is one part of our faith in God. Biblical authority is part of a faith-attitude. And this means one thing above all: when a portion of scripture speaks to us, the question for us is not primarily 'Is this in itself, as a piece of historical narrative perhaps, or as a piece of doctrine, or as a piece of moral wisdom, simply valid and true?' but: 'In what way does this material, whether doctrinal, narrative, or moral, fit in with the problem of faith in Jesus Christ and the doing of his will, and in what way does it serve the upbuilding of faith and the learning of that obedience?' The authority of the Bible lies within the total faith-relation of man with Christ. This means, in particular, that it does not rest upon any values or virtues perceptible from a vantage-point without that faith-relation. The Bible may, or may not, be good or great literature; it may, or may not, be accurate in its historical indications; it may, or may not, display a powerfully coherent world-view – and for all these things one would probably have to say that what is true of one part of the Bible is not true of another. But, even granting the maximum possible to the virtues of the Bible as literature, or as history, or as expression of a coherent world-view, none of these provide the *basis* for the authority of the Bible. And conversely, even if it is shockingly bad as literature, or quite erratic as history, or untenable as world-view, – or dubious as science if it comes to that – none of these should seriously affect the basis of its authority, though by taking them into consideration we may be helped to understand better the *nature* of that authority. But the *basis* of that authority lies in its efficacy in the faith-relation between man and God.

But, you may well say at this point, this is all very well, but how does all this work? Is this not a sort of theoretical position which leaves vague the answer to all the questions people are actually asking? Well, perhaps so: I wanted to begin by stating a position, and then on the basis of this we can look at many of the individual questions. So let us now fill this out by taking up several of the questions that people are likely to ask.

One reaction might be to say that I have claimed too much: by saying that the Bible is built up into the structure of Christian faith, am I suggesting that in order to be a Christian one must 'believe the Bible', as people put it, that one must, simply by being a Christian, accept as factual and correct and theologically valid everything that is to be found within the pages of this volume? The result would then be that one had either to accept everything as the Bible tells it – creation in seven days, changing of water into wine, the 969 years that Methuselah lived, and so on – or else admit that one could not be Christian. One would have then, to use the rough terminology people use, to choose between being a fundamentalist and being an atheist. Well, of course, that is not what I mean. In talking about the essential *implication* of scripture in the process of salvation, in the life of the church, and in the faith of the Christian, we are not talking about 'accepting' the contents of the Bible or 'believing the Bible'. Christian faith is not faith in the Bible, not primarily: it is faith in Christ as the one through whom one comes to God, and faith that through the Bible we meet him, he communicates with us. The Bible is thus the instrument of faith and the expression of faith, rather than the object of faith. Thus, in particular, our recognition that the Bible provides an essential and God-given meeting-ground for our encounter with God in faith does not alter the fact that we have a right, and indeed a duty, to use the Bible *critically*. In using the word 'critically' I am not referring in the first place to biblical criticism, as usually so termed, e.g. to the idea that the Pentateuch was written not by Moses but by three or four different sources that were later combined, though that is not an inconsiderable portion of what I intend. I mean more specifically that the sayings of scripture have to be weighed and measured by us, reverently indeed – because all of this material comes from profound wrestling with God in fear and faith – but also critically. The Bible does not have the property of perfection, which belongs only to God himself. It is not part of the Christian faith that the Bible furnishes a depiction of God possessing the maximum possible accuracy. Or, to put it in another way, the Bible as such is not the source or the foundation of Christian belief. It is our relation with Christ that is the foundation of the church. It is the message of good news, the gospel of grace, that is the source and the foundation of faith. If it were not so, as a matter of fact, there would have never been any Bible: the Bible came into existence because there were men of faith who believed on the ground of God's promises and his grace, at a time when there was as yet no Bible, and who created the Bible as the written crystallization of their experience and their tradition. In a real sense the men of the Bible had no Bible: there was no Bible in the biblical period. Abraham believed God not because he read about it in the Bible but because he heard his voice and followed him in faith. Faith's relationship to God, which is primary, gives the right and also the means for a reverently critical use of the material of scripture. It is thus in principle perfectly possible, not only to question the scientific or the historical accuracy of various biblical passages, but also to question the adequacy of the picture of God which they present. To do this is not to derogate from the authority of scripture: on the contrary, it is often to apply it – for in most cases the person who questions the adequacy of the depiction of God in one biblical passage is doing so on the basis of another biblical passage, and this is in fact the way in which the function of biblical authority exercises itself.

But there is another objection which comes from a different angle, and goes somewhat as follows: even granted all this, granted that scripture was closely involved in the process of salvation, granted that faith does not mean assent to each and every biblical assertion, how can it make so much difference anyway? Not just odd bits of the Bible, which might be critically handled and brought into place, but the whole thing, all of it together, comes from an ancient world and belongs to a universe of meaning that we today no longer share, so that even if it is all true and can all be weighed and appreciated correctly it cannot possibly tell us today what we should think or believe. This is the argument that can be described for short as that of cultural relativism. Opinions are relative to the culture in which they are formed. The New Testament, for instance, it may be argued, originated in a world deeply convinced of the reality of demon possession: it was also profoundly concerned by the fear of death and the question whether immortality might be gained. There were, equally, certain preconceptions about the relation between soul and body. A great deal that is said in the New Testament is predicated upon these assumptions. But in our culture, today, these assumptions no longer hold good, indeed they are so far from us that they have simply no meaning at all: it is just impossible therefore that documents which make these assumptions can be meaningful, much less authoritative, for us today.

Now this position is by no means easy to counter. For the present purpose I would like to reply in two ways. First of all, the cultural relativism argument goes too far in separating one stage of culture from another. Cultures are not encapsulated entities, in which nothing is intelligible except for the dominant assumptions of the particular culture now existing. It is normal in a culture to have a memory of the past, so that the remembered past is part of the culture; and this is especially so where those much earlier stages are made available to us through classic written documents, such as the Greek and Latin classics to the humanist or the Bible to Jewish and Christian societies. We can and do read books about a world which is no longer our world: doing so is a normal part of the educational process. We can understand a book about a world infested with evil spirits even if we do not experience such a world ourselves. And such a reading establishes a historical contact with the past. Through the Bible we know that we have a historical continuity with these people who experienced evil spirits everywhere, and we know that in a sense we belong together with them.

Moreover, from this point of view the Bible is not one single culture: it is a stream of slowly altering cultures, spread out over more than a thousand years. Exactly these things which I have mentioned, fear of death, longing for immortality, conceptions of soul and body, power of evil spirits, which were so marked in the first-century environment of early Christianity were lacking in large sections of the Old Testament, so that on these particular points the Old Testament seems closer to modern culture than the New. The Bible is a spectrum of cultures rather than one particular narrow band of culture. And of course the men of the New Testament, little as was their sense for historical investigation, had their own horizons immensely enlarged by their possession of the Old Testament, which placed their frontiers in Mesopotamia and in Egypt, in the reign of Nebuchadnezzar and in the Persian Empire.

The final argument against the cultural relativist position is one that follows from something I said earlier, when I stressed that the authority of the Bible lay in the meeting with Christ which it mediated, and not in the acceptance as true of the information or attitudes which it contained. The authority of scripture does not mean that, because the world of the gospels was full of evil spirits, we must see evil spirits of the same sort, doing the same kind of evil, in our world today: maybe we should see them, maybe we should not, but biblical authority leaves it open whether we see them or not. It never should have been our view of biblical authority, that it meant that all the cultural baggage of past ages should be loaded upon the unfortunate bearer of the twentieth century.

But, then, let us pass to another form of the question, and ask ourselves: why after all *the Bible?* Why this book, or rather this collection of books, and not some other? Does it just happen accidentally to be the Bible that is authoritative, or is there some *reason* for the centrality which we have been ascribing to it? For the Bible did not drop from heaven, a divine book ready-made by God. God did not sing the Psalms to Israel, Israel sang them to God. St Paul wrote his letters to the churches of this place and that.

As we know today, the Bible is the product of a long process of formation and revision of *traditions.* The traditions were the memories and the instructions which were passed down in various authoritative channels: circles of prophets and story-tellers, of priests, of wise men, of apostles and men who had been with Jesus. These traditions were the traditions of the people of God, both in its form as Israel and in its form as the church of Jesus Christ. The Bible, the written documents, forms the final precipitate from this long fluid state of tradition. Gradually the spoken traditions crystallized into a particular form, the processes of editing, compiling and redaction drew towards a close, books came to be formed, and these were holy scriptures. Traditions came before scriptures, and scriptures came before the Bible: for 'the Bible' implies a fixed and closed collection, and this was not reached until a very late stage when a so-called 'canon' of scripture was drawn up. Within biblical terms themselves this was not yet so: there was, finally, vir-tually one 'canon', i.e. the one book of the Pentateuch, probably another of the Prophets; beyond this it is quite doubtful whether the Writings were yet clearly defined in scope. Books were not bound together in one volume, each book was a separate scroll, a physical fact which makes quite a difference to the definitional question. Most early Christians did not know four gospels, most of them no doubt knew only one; the really early ones perhaps did not know any. 'Canon', as the principle of a fixed and closed collection, is very late, long after biblical times.

Now the formation of written scriptures did not bring to an end the formation of church tradition, just as it had not brought to an end the new formation of Jewish tradition. What the existence of scripture did was to alter the character of post-scriptural tradition. First of all, the existence of a holy and authoritative scripture, even if its boundaries were inexact, caused all other tradition from the biblical period to disappear. The Jews had practically no authentic tradition from older biblical times other than the biblical books themselves: all the books to which they make reference, the Book of the Wars of the Lord and the Book of the Chronicles of the Kings of Judah and the like, have become unknown. We similarly have practically no information about Jesus that came down from first-century Christians, other than what is contained in the New Testament. Scripture thus came to have an almost exclusive position as the sole authentic source coming from the biblical period, i.e., as expressing the deliberate and explicit voice of the men of that time, their message, their story, which they wanted to leave as their final message, from the end of the biblical development, to later ages. But, secondly, the presence of scripture altered the character of post-scriptural tradition. In essence that tradition by its own will became exegetical. It itself assumed an interpretative function in relation to that antecedent segment of tradition, the segment now represented by the written scriptures, which it itself now accepted as source and authority. Thus in a way if one asks why the Bible should be taken as authoritative in relation to the later growth and development of Christianity, the answer is that that decision was in fact taken long ago and has thus long been built into the structure of Christianity. The acceptance of scripture as something different in function from other tradition has been made by that other tradition itself.

Now, from this we can go on to ask, is there some further reason behind all this, or is it just a mere accident that certain materials came to be regarded as 'holy scripture' and thereby different from other tradition? Is there something in these books themselves that gives them authority, and if so what is it?

The tendency of modern theology has been to explain the authority of the Bible through its reference to past events. God

revealed himself in the past, in past events, and biblical narratives report this revelation, or witness to it, or interpret it. This
belongs to a doctrine of *antecedent* revelation: revelation precedes the scripture, just as it precedes the church.

But, as we have just seen, scripture certainly does not have
a place antecedent to the church (in 'church' I include ancient
Israel). Scripture emerged from the tradition of the people of
God. Instead of the traditional model which reads something
like God → revelation → scripture → church we should have a
newer model which would read something like God → people
→ tradition → scripture, with revelation attached to no one
place specifically but rather deriving from all the stages alike.

Let us put it this way: our view of scripture has been too
much dominated by *the past*. I want to suggest that the functioning of the Bible is much more directed towards *the future*. It
is often said that Christianity is a historical religion, and that is
in many ways true, though it is a much more vague and uncertain assertion than is commonly understood; but, if it means
that Christianity works in the milieu of human historical experience, that milieu exists not only in the direction of the arrow
pointing towards the past but also in the direction pointing
towards the future. That Christianity is an eschatological
religion, looking towards the future fulfilment of God's promise
to mankind, is just as important as that it is a historical religion
looking back to certain foundational events.

Now this, if valid, is important for several of the questions
we have been discussing. First of all, it is important for the
direction of the interpretative process. Everyone knows that the
Bible is an ancient book. Much of our interpretative striving has
been directed towards the task of making the meaning of that
ancient book lucid and relevant for the present day, i.e., you
take the past meaning of the Bible and seek to transfer it into
the present day, to make it clear, bright and meaningful today.
But it is doubtful whether this can be done or whether when
done it is as rich in results as one would hope. Perhaps we
should look in the other direction and say that it is not the Bible
that needs to be elucidated for the present day, but the present
day that needs to be elucidated in the light of the Bible. The
Bible is not a book, reporting on what to it was already past,
that has then to be dragged into a much later present: rather,
it is a book that, though on a first level narrating the past, on
a deeper level was speaking of the future and for the future.

Quite a lot of the narrative material of the Bible can be seen in this way. While on the surface narrating the past, the interest of the writers was often in the present and the future. Stories about Abraham were told, not in order to inform the reader of how things had been in the second millennium, but in order to give pictures of the way in which the promise of God, which was yet to come, had been fulfilled – and therefore of how, for others much later, it might be fulfilled. The prophetic books were compiled and edited into their present form, not in order to give an accurate historical picture of what prophets at such and such a time had said, but to depict the working of the word of God and offer patterns of the way in which it would again and again work in human affairs. Likewise, the story of Jesus, as told in the gospels, may be a mixture of historical narrative, which tells what he said and did, and paradigmatic interpretation, which provides and sets forth a way in which the Christians of the future will have to understand him. To seek to prove that these stories fit in with their historical setting and are therefore accurate, as if such fitting with the historical setting was the ground for their authenticity and authority, is thus to miss the point entirely: to seek to ground the authority of the Bible in its accuracy as past history is often to break down its real authority altogether. Scripture is not in essence a 'record'; and it is not at all difficult to see that its authority may be maintained even while the historical accuracy of its narrative reports is seen to be quite variable.

What then about the question of the parts as against the whole? Does the authority of the Bible mean the authority of the whole, or the authority of every part? Is there a difference of emphasis as between one part of the Bible and another? – or does one have to take the whole thing as one piece? Does one go by the general impression of the whole, or does one have to take all the details seriously? Well, the question divides into several parts. From one point of view, the detail of the Bible is supremely important. The Bible is like a picture: the marginal details do not dominate the picture, but if the details were different the picture as a whole would be different. And let it not be imagined that the details are the resort of the obscurantist and fundamentalist mind: on the contrary, it is through taking seriously the details of the Bible that the great critical solutions, like the discernment of the sources of the Pentateuch or the interrelationships between the various gospels, were achieved.

Yet on the other hand this does not mean that all parts of the Bible provide equally vivid and equally complete depictions of God and his will; I don't think that they do. Some things are more central, some more marginal. Some books are more central than others: Isaiah is more central than Ecclesiastes or the Song of Songs, Romans is more central than II Timothy or II Peter – few people really deny this. The themes and the content are closer to the major religious message of the Bible, closer to the gospel as we might call it. To say this is not to down-grade the others: what is less central nevertheless retains its importance in determining the balance of the whole and the make-up of the mass of detail.

There are, I think, two aspects that remain to be discussed before I conclude. Firstly, if we talk of the authority of the Bible in the ways I have outlined, one might put the question: authority over what? How does this authority work? Does biblical authority mean that on every question one has to begin from the Bible, that nothing can be accepted unless it has a biblical foundation? And how does it all apply to questions that are not so much of doctrine as of ethics and daily life? For instance, what can the Bible say that is authoritative over the question of euthanasia, or nuclear weapons? Such questions are, of course, not directly treated by the Bible. Some people think we should derive from the Bible *principles* which can then be applied to decision about these matters – that is to say, a primarily rationalist procedure. I would put it in this way: the authority of the Bible does not operate inductively, that is, we do not derive from the Bible information that in itself authorizes or gives the foundation for such and such a doctrinal or ethical position. Rather, our doctrinal and ethical positions have as their point of origin a total vision, a conception of what Christian life, action and society should be like. These visions come from Christian men, informed by the Bible but also informed by all sorts of other influences which play upon their lives: actually many of the beliefs which are most adamantly defended on the grounds of their biblical basis cannot be derived from the Bible at all, for instance the idea that the inspiration of scripture is a guard against historical error and is the foundation of faith and practice. But, in respect of these visions of church and society, the Bible exercises a critical role: it questions what people think, it queries the basis of their judgments, it asks whether the tradition which modern men form is really in continuity with its biblical origins. It is through this checking and questioning role that the Bible exercises its authority: the Bible queries the tradition of its own interpretation.

Finally, I mentioned just above the matter of divine inspiration. Many people over a long time have thought that the authority of the Bible rested above all upon divine inspiration, and that this meant above all the prevention of any sort of error. I have just indicated how thin is the evidence, within the Bible itself, for any such belief: the famous text in which inspiration is mentioned, II Tim. 3.16, is from a fairly marginal source, and it makes no connection whatever between inspiration and historical accuracy, it leaves it quite vague which books were the 'scriptures' under discussion, and above all it is notable for its low-key treatment of the matter: though it says that all scriptures is inspired, it does not for a moment suggest that this is the foundation of Christian doctrine or practice, all it says is that scripture, being inspired, is 'profitable' for doctrine, for reproof, for correction, for instruction in righteousness. In other words, the inspiration of scripture, as defined in this famous text, has nothing to do with the accuracy of scripture or its primacy as the foundation of all doctrine, it is concerned with its practical effects as a 'useful' source of moral correction.

Nevertheless there is no reason why we should not continue to use the term *inspiration* if we find it useful, and if we do so I think it has to be used in the following sense. We have seen that scripture emerged from the tradition of the people of God. Now there is no reason why we should say that the scripture, i.e. the final written product, is inspired by God but the stages which led up to it, in which the important decisions were taken, the stages of oral tradition and the like, were not inspired by God. So inspiration would have to be understood in the sense that God in his Spirit was in and with his people in the formation, transmission, writing down and completion of their tradition and its completion and fixation as scripture. In this process the final stage, the final fixation, was the least important rather than the most important. Now this helps us with another question: is the authority really the authority of the books as books, or is it the authority of the persons who wrote the books and the persons about whom they are written? Do we believe Romans because, being scripture, it is authoritative, or do we believe it because it was by St Paul who as a person was authoritative? In the way I have put the matter, it is not necessary to make the choice an absolute one. Authority resides in the people of God, or perhaps more correctly in the central leadership of the people of God; but it also resides in the scripture which they formed and passed on to later generations as their own communication, as the voice which they wanted to be heard as their voice. The grounding of scripture is in the history of tradition within Israel and the earliest church. In such a sense it seems to me possible that the hallowed term 'inspiration of scripture' can be revitalized and re-used for our own time. But if this was to be done, it would have to be made clear that inspiration of this sort had nothing to do with the guaranteeing of historical accuracy or with infallibility of any other kind. It would be a theological affirmation of the faith that God had been with his people in their formation of the thoughts, memories and instructions which finally came to constitute our Bible.

It is not possible in one lecture to touch on all aspects of the question of biblical authority for today, but I hope that I have looked at some of the major areas of uncertainty; and I hope to have suggested some possible ways in which, in the midst of the many pressures of modern thought and life, we can still confidently reaffirm that the Bible has authority within the church and is able to speak to us as a message that reaches us from God.

5

The Problem of Fundamentalism Today

This subject is a very complex one, and in a single lecture I cannot do more than summarize a few aspects of it. For greater detail and comprehensiveness I have to refer to my book *Fundamentalism*.[1] In this paper I want to confine myself to the following aspects: the basic character of fundamentalism, the nature of the criticisms I have myself advanced against it, some facets of the ensuing discussion, and in particular the role of conservative scholarship in relation to the religious core of fundamentalism. Here and there I will take into account the reviews I have seen,[2] the discussions I have had since my book was published, and various other books recently published.

But let us begin by outlining what the general limits of fundamentalism are. One may start by saying not what fundamentalism is, but what is not. It is not, to my mind, fundamentalism if one thinks that the Bible and its doctrine should be the absolute controlling authority, under God and under Jesus Christ, of the doctrine of the church and the practice of Christians. To ascribe such final authority to scripture is not fundamentalism. Such a position, which may go so far as to state the nature of authority in the church in terms of scripture alone, may have its difficulties; but it remains a position that can be perfectly well maintained within the main stream of Christianity and it does not constitute fundamentalism. Fundamentalism begins when people begin to say that the doctrinal and practical authority of scripture is necessarily tied to its infallibility and in particular its historical inerrancy, when they maintain that its doctrinal and practical authority will stand up *only* if it is in general without error, and this means in particular only if it is without error in its apparently historical remarks. The centre of fundamentalism is the insistence that the control of doctrine and practice by scripture is dependent on something like a general perfection of scripture, and therefore on its historical inerrancy; and this in turn involves the repudiation of the results of modern critical modes of reading the Bible.

Now the broader religious context of this lies in certain currents of Protestantism. In the Anglo-Saxon world the central and dominant context is that of Evangelicalism, the revivalist movement of the eighteenth and nineteenth centuries with its emphasis on personal faith and religion, personal new birth – the tradition of Wesley, Whitefield, Moody, Billy Graham. This tradition, for all its strong conviction, was to some extent theologically eclectic: it had no first-rate theological thinkers, and it did not identify itself absolutely with any of the traditional denominational theologies. If one wing of it was Calvinist, another was Arminian, and on the whole the Arminian wing was the dominant one. Outside the Anglo-Saxon world, however, much fundamentalism came from a root that lay earlier in the history of the church: it lay rather in the traditional denominational orthodoxies of the seventeenth centuries. We can see this, for instance, in the Missouri Synod of American Lutheranism, which has recently shown so extreme an outburst of fundamentalist ideology in the case of Concordia Seminary, with the consequent birth of Christ Seminary (Seminex = Seminary in Exile); and similarly in various churches of Dutch and German Reformed origins. In these cases fundamentalism is associated with a traditional scholastic and confessional orthodoxy. These two streams of conservative Protestantism, one going back to revivalism, the other to older confessional orthodoxy, have often run parallel and supported one another. But the difference in emphasis and in context remains important.

The difference between these two forms a source of tension within conservative and fundamentalist Christianity. It is beyond doubt that much popular fundamentalism has been theologically weak and in scholarly regards naive. On the other hand I myself think that the old fundamentalists of the Anglo-Saxon world were in many ways right in their decision (taken no doubt unconsciously) to reassert a Christianity that could be communicated by the common man and that was in essence personal, dependent on personal faith now present in the believer, as against the traditional denominational orthodoxies. For it is an elementary insight of true evangelical faith that there is such a thing as dead orthodoxy and that conformity to an orthodox norm does not constitute true faith. (In this sense, incidentally, it should be emphasized that my arguments against fundamentalism are not at all anti-evangelical in character; on the contrary, they seek to maintain one of the primary interests and concerns of all true evangelical faith against the zeal for orthodoxy which can so easily stifle it.) It is therefore all the more unhappy that in modern Anglo-Saxon conservative evangelicalism the aspiration to orthodoxy seems to be increasing and leaders are seeking to foist a traditional Dutch Calvinism or some other such doctrinal position upon the evangelical movement. It would not have been possible for evangelical and fundamentalist Christianity to carry out the immensely important missionary work that it did in the nineteenth century if it had insisted on remaining tied in detail to the traditional denominational theologies. Fundamentalism represents a coalition between various groups; but it was from those who cherished traditional orthodoxy that the intellectual leadership came, and notably of course from Warfield.

As we all know, fundamentalism is not anyone's ideal: people do not aspire to be called fundamentalists and do not call themselves by this name with pride. The ideal to which they aspire is rather that of the evangelical, or for others that of the orthodox Lutheran or Calvinist. If you read the modern evangelical periodicals, often quite pleasant journals like *Sojourners*, you see that 'evangelical' is the word they never tire of, it occurs in almost every paragraph, it is the desired identity, endlessly repeated. But for many, if 'evangelical' or 'orthodox' is the desired identity, the *ideology* remains the fundamentalist one. Though there may be, and are, many evangelicals and many orthodox who are not fundamentalists, there is little sign that they have or seek to have a strong and independent position about the Bible to set against the fundamentalist one. Conservative evangelicals seem mostly to hold the main points of the fundamentalist position, conceding only minor modifications; under strain and pressure from critics they will try to display a more open position, but left to themselves they will fall back on a fundamentalist position, modified as little as possible. Thus fundamentalism has a power and an influence extending far beyond the numbers of those who are actual fundamentalists.

Thus nothing material is to be achieved by listing the names of persons or organizations which are, or are not, fundamen-

talist. Fundamentalists are usually very anxious not to be identified by that name; indeed, one might say that anxiety to avoid
the name of 'fundamentalist' is a fairly good index that a person
is rather close to being one. Fundamentalists, on the whole, do
not think that there are any fundamentalists at all: if there are,
they are very extreme, very few in number, and very far away,
usually in another country. But all this does not alter the powerful, pervasive, and easily identifiable character of the ideology
which other Christians identify as fundamentalism; and there
is no reason why those who maintain that ideology in its fuller
form should not be classified as fundamentalists. Probably more
important, however, is the influence of the fundamentalist
ideology upon those who accept it only in part.

Now the kernel of my own position can be presented as
follows. Conservatism is a human ideology; and religious conservatism is also a human ideology. As human ideologies such
conservatisms may have much justification, and they may well
be just as well founded as the opposing liberal ideologies. It is
important therefore that in criticising fundamentalism we do
not simply stand as propagators of liberalism.[3] Conservatism,
as I have said, when taken purely as human ideology is not an
entirely intolerable or unjustifiable position and one can easily
see salutary functions which it can perform, just as one can see
salutary functions which liberalism may perform. But, when
endowed with a religious sanction and made into the kernel of
the message of scripture, or the support upon which the message of scripture is thought to depend, conservatism becomes
demonic. Conservative evangelicalism and fundamentalism are
doctrinal and religious positions which seek to tie Christian
faith indissolubly to conservative ideology: their doctrines of
scripture and scriptural infallibility are devices which ensure
that scripture will speak only in terms of this conservative ideology. Seeking to protect the authority of scripture, they have in
fact imposed upon scripture a human religious tradition; and,
seeking to elevate scripture, they have in fact deeply distorted
its meaning. The only way we can recover the sense of scripture
today is by asking what it really means. It is the critical study
of scripture, and the critical theology which accompanies it, that
does this; it is conservative evangelicalism and fundamentalism
that seek to prevent this from being done.

Now in my book I shifted the analysis of fundamentalism in
several central respects away from the picture of it that has

been customary in mainstream Christianity. It is interesting, but to me not surprising, that conservative reviews and replies have paid little attention to these shifts of emphasis. On two essential points, which I shall mention, I offered a diagnosis of fundamentalism that was more charitable and favourable towards it than is common opinion in the churches. Firstly, I eschewed the view, commonly held, that fundamentalism is essentially based on emotion and that it refuses to allow the intellect to play upon the verities of the Christian religion. Secondly, I resolutely refused to use the psychological argument, to argue, that is, that the basis of fundamentalism is to be sought in a bigoted, authoritarian, security-seeking personality structure. This is, after all, what most Christians think: but I think it is a deeply insulting assessment of another Christian tradition. Now let us look first of all at the psychological argument. For abandoning the use of this argument, I received little or no recognition or thanks from evangelical reviewers. Since then I have discussed the matter personally with several of them, and their feelings were deeply interesting. They felt no gratitude for my abstention from use of the psychological argument, because they in their own experience felt that that argument is often valid: they themselves, as conservatives working within the conservative evangelical world, feel the pressure of what seems to them to be an inherent psychological stress. So maybe most people are right, and I was wrong to eschew the psychological argument. Yet I do not feel it so: it seems to me that the doctrine produces the psychology, not the psychology the doctrine. Young evangelical Christians, open, free and delightful, are often quickly reduced through the life of their society and the pressure of their doctrine to a strained, suspicious and exclusivist frame of mind, and this is a familiar experience to anyone with experience of the movement. These are not people who were inherently bigoted or who had from the beginning a pathological personality structure. They did not begin this way: it was fundamentalism that made them this way.

But I come back to the first point: the place of intellect and reason in fundamentalism. Of course, these observers are not entirely wrong who have said that fundamentalism refuses to allow the intellect to play upon the substance of the Christian religion. But this is not for the reason commonly given, namely that fundamentalism is basically emotional; and, even if it was so, it is not clear to me that a religious current can be properly criticized merely for being emotional: the question would seem to be rather, what is the quality of the emotions involved? As I have depicted it, fundamentalism is basically an intellectual system, but an intellectual system of such a kind that it deprives the intellect of power to do much constructively about the faith. Its function is to create a space within which a particular religious tradition, with its doctrines, its emotions, and its traditional interpretations of scripture, along with its traditional language, habits and social organization, may continue unchanged and in strength; but the means by which it performs this function are essentially intellectual. If we start from the old distinction between fideism, an approach based on the primacy of faith, and rationalism, an approach based on the primacy of reason, though fundamentalism seems to many at first sight to be a fideist position, it is actually a rationalist position; indeed, it is perhaps the only really rationalist position widely operative within Christianity today. It is because of the strong heritage of rationalism in the English-speaking cultural tradition that fundamentalism is at its strongest in the Anglo-Saxon world. Nowhere is the rationalism of fundamentalist argument more clear than in the doctrine of the inspiration and infallibility of the Bible itself. Though inspiration is mentioned in the Bible, nowhere does the Bible suggest that inspiration includes the package of implications taken as authoritative by fundamentalists: it nowhere says that this implies historical accuracy, it nowhere says anything about the original autographs, indeed it nowhere says that Jesus commanded or authorized the writing of the New Testament at all. The fundamentalist construction is not derived from what scripture actually says but is derived *rationally*: the fundamentalist as a rational man cannot see how the scripture can be inspired unless it is historically inerrant. Fundamentalism is of course not an *unbelieving* rationalism, and it is indeed against such an unbelieving rationalism that its basic polemic is directed; but it remains a rationalism all the same. It is thus not surprising that fundamentalism in many cultures is a middle-class rather than a popular movement: it is a tolerably educated movement, including in its ranks plenty of doctors, scientists, lawyers and most of all of course students; and it is from this stratum that the basic spread of ideological doctrine takes place. But fundamentalism has never understood the opponents, against whom its polemic is directed, well enough to realize that they do not hold a rationalism at all:

fundamentalism, as I say, is the one solidly rationalistic position prominent in modern Christianity.

In discussion with fundamentalists and their sympathizers, such as one has after a book like my own is published, nothing is more evident than the craving of fundamentalists for *intellectual* confirmation and justification. Critics of a book like mine do not argue much from faith or from scripture: they argue from intellectual capacity. Those who have written books critical of fundamentalism are represented as ill-informed ignoramuses. In this I personally followed a long line of earlier ignoramuses, such as Gabriel Hebert and Michael Ramsey. The fact that I scarcely mentioned John Stott or F. F. Bruce was delightedly hailed as evidence that I knew nothing of these great men. It was repeatedly suggested that I knew no evangelical literature other than the limited amount cited in my bibliography, though that amount might seem enough to most people. Even fundamentalist controversialists might have stopped to think that there might be other reasons why I mentioned no more. But this is the way in which fundamentalists and their supporters approach the matter. It is, when one looks at the conservative reviews, as if they had just got together and said: all we need to do is to show that he does not know his facts.[4] As one of my correspondents so vividly put it, 'You proffessors do not know nothing' (*sic*). The craving for intellectual justification, including attacks on the intellectual validity of the thinking and work of non-conservative writers, is central and normal to the fundamentalist approach to reality. But, as I shall show, the real situation is quite a lot different: and it is the evangelical constituency that often fails to know, or to take into account, what is being thought by the scholarly leadership which it itself reveres.

The very craving of fundamentalists for intellectual justification is itself evidence of a deep intellectual self-distrust. There can, of course, be great learning and perfectly good scholarship allied with extremely conservative religious views. Fundamentalists continually quote the names of conservative scholars and apparently derive comfort from the fact that such persons exist. And, of course, on any particular question there is a valid more conservative path to follow, just as there is a valid more radical or more adventurous path to follow. A conservative view can be a salutary caution against rash innovations or hasty critical decisions. My own exegetical leanings are in fact conservative in just this sense. But the fundamentalist constituency deeply misunderstands the meaning and the value of the conservative scholarship which it so deeply venerates and so endlessly cites.

In fact the scholarship deemed conservative and venerated by fundamentalists is deeply ambiguous in its relation to their own religious and doctrinal concerns. For the fundamentalist, the existence of conservative scholarship functions as a sort of propaganda. It does not mean that he intends to adjust his own view of the Bible, or of possible interplay with critical scholarship, to the views that conservative scholars hold or to the way in which they interact with more critical colleagues. On the contrary, conservative scholarship functions as a signal of confirmation, giving him encouragement to go on on his way as he has done in the past. It creates an intellectual space within which the fundamentalist society can continue just as it was before. A conversation with a fundamentalist or a conservative evangelical seldom lasts more than ten seconds before some conservative scholar, often a good friend and long-time colleague of my own, is cited. This is done because they think that such a scholar is on their side and his existence thus gives them intellectual encouragement. This does not mean that they intend to adjust and modify their doctrine or understanding of scripture in order to take into account the positions accepted by such a scholar in his professional work. The conservative scholar is not quoted because the fundamentalist is willing to adjust to what that scholar thinks: he is quoted because it is supposed that his mere existence justifies the fundamentalist in continuing as he was before.

Secondly, fundamentalists in their own appeal to conservative scholarship show that they do not understand what scholarship is about, and they thus work to corrupt the true values of the very scholars they respect. As has been admitted, there are conservative and fundamentalist scholars of great learning. Their work is, or may be, creative especially in those areas in which there is little or no clash with a critical approach to scripture: in general, the ancillary fields, in contrast with exegesis proper. There are brains, then, to be found in the fundamentalist camp, or at least supposed to be on that side: have I not argued all along that it is in essence an intellectual system? But – and here is the difference – the essence of scholarship does not lie in brains or learning: it lies in ideas, in fresh analysis, in new perspectives. On this side even the best conservative scholarship is shockingly defective. It is stodgy, apologetic and uncreative. Its dullness is monumental. What striking new line of approach, what creative new method, what fresh analysis has ever come from it, even in its most creditable modern forms? In so far as any newer ideas are to be heard, from time to time, within conservative scholarship – lines, for example, deriving from structuralism, from modern linguistics, from the so-called 'New Hermeneutic' – these, whether good or bad, are approaches which were developed outside conservatism and were taken over by it only later, usually because it was fancied that some conservative advantage could be gained from doing so; often, as with form criticism, redaction criticism and the like, they are approaches which were actually developed only in the teeth of bitter conservative resistance. And this lack of ideas in conservative scholarship – however respectable the intellectual talents employed in it – is not so very surprising. For, if there is a sector of scholarship that is really conservative, that wants to show that the Bible really means just what it was believed in the seventeenth or eighteenth centuries to mean, before modern scholarship started out, then of course such scholarship will not probably be fertile in new ideas. Quantity of learning is one thing, and the presence of creative imagination is another. Rationalism and imagination conflict with one another: the striking absence of conservative evangelical creativity in *literature*, particularly in contrast with catholic strains of Christianity, is not accidental. Conservatism thus tends to put a premium on quantity of learning rather than on freshness of analysis; and this proportion is easily visible in modern conservative evangelical scholarly literature, in English at least. And this leads us to the proper answer to a question which I find often put to me: why is it that conservative text-books are not more often recommended as reading by professors in non-conservative institutions? Is it not fair that all points of view should have a hearing? Well, if one wants to study points of view about the Bible then of course conservative evangelical literature must be considered, whether good or bad, and on this principle one would wish to recommend equal quantities of Roman Catholic, Greek Orthodox, Unitarian, Jewish, atheistic and other materials, so as to get the point of view of all. But for serious study of the Bible it is quality in ideas that should and must count, rather than representation of a point of view. If students want to hear a point of view, then conservative evangelical literature will do that excellently for them: but if they want their minds to be stirred and the currents of new insights to become visible to them, then conservative literature will seldom perform that function.

And this leads on to another point. The partisan light in which fundamentalists regard conservative scholarship itself corrupts the path which that scholarship may take. Partisan scholarship is of no use as scholarship: the only worthwhile criterion for scholarship is that it should be good scholarship, not that it should be conservative scholarship or any other kind of scholarship. And many conservative scholars realize this very well. Among their non-conservative peers they do not produce the arguments that fundamentalist opinion considers essential and they do not behave in the way that the fundamentalist society requires of its members. Fundamentalist apologists, exasperated, often ask me the question: but how can the conservative scholar win? Is not the balance loaded against him? The answer is: yes, he can win, but he can win only if he approaches the Bible not as a conservative or as an evangelical scholar, but as a scholar of the biblical text. The partisan use to which conservative and fundamentalist society puts its own favoured segment of scholarship itself destroys the value of that which that scholarship may rightly have to offer.

It is therefore not by accident, but arises from the nature of the case, that even the conservative scholar, when talking outside his own fundamentalist constituency, usually talks in the same language as the critical scholar. I do not say that he shares the same presuppositions, for he very likely does not: but as a rule he conceals his presuppositions, for he knows very well that, if he sets them in the forefront, he will only depreciate the value of his own scholarly work. Thus conservative scholars share the same general universe of discourse with the rest of the academic community to which they belong, and they do so in a way which their own fundamentalist constituency does not understand and could not accept if it did so. In saying this I do not say that critical methods are used: this may or may not be so. I simply say that the general mode of reasoning used by the scholars whom fundamentalists accept and revere is on the same level as that used by critical scholars. What the conservative scholar does not do is to communicate this fact when he is talking to his own fundamentalist constituency.

Thus, to sum up this point, the existence of conservative scholarship is much more ambivalent in relation to fundamentalist religious society than is generally realized. The value and acclaim attached to it is a sign of the rationalist and intellectualist emphasis which is so obvious in fundamentalist thinking. In fact, however, the scholars who are so venerated by fundamentalists are frequently, whether consciously or tacitly, very much at odds with fundamentalist society. Sometimes indeed they do good work in providing means to lighten the burden of fundamentalist strictness and to defend younger scholars against the restrictions which it would impose if left to itself.

In this paper I have talked several times of fundamentalist 'society'. Something more should now be said about this. In many countries, such as Great Britain, it is typical that denominations contain a fundamentalist element, and not that any particular church or denomination should be identified as being in itself fundamentalist. Thus many fundamentalists co-exist with other Christians in a large church; on the other hand, particular parishes or congregations may be traditionally fundamentalist and remain so over long periods of time. Moreover, there are well-known fundamentalist inter-denominational organizations, which often follow a rigid partisan line, expressed most clearly in the choice of speakers and leaders; and such organizations often have extensive publishing activities, which strongly support an orthodox and more or less fundamentalist line. There is also, however, the situation of what I have called 'culture fundamentalism', where a more or less fundamentalist religion extends fairly uniformly over a wide area of society.

The social character of fundamentalism is of the greatest importance for the understanding of its functioning, for it is basic to its ethical stance. By this I do not refer to the common alliance between fundamentalism and political-social conservatism, though that is not without importance. This aspect, though often identified as central by critics of fundamentalist religion, is not in my opinion either invariable or absolutely central. By an 'ethical stance' I mean something else. I mean that the real problem of fundamentalists is the way in which they regard and estimate other people, people who stand outside the fundamentalist society. From the way in which fundamentalists present the matter one would often suppose that the criticism of their position by mainstream Christianity is predominantly an intellectual criticism: that is, fundamentalists feel that others despise them for lack of intellectual ability and integrity, and precisely in reaction to this they often fall victim to intellectual boasting and (very ill-founded) intellectual self-satisfaction. In my judgment the real criticism of fundamentalism is not an intellectual one of this sort, but rather an ethical one. The Pauline argument, that among true believers not many are intellectually gifted, is to me a very powerful and valid one, though one hears very little of it from modern conservative apologists. The real fault in fundamentalism is not its lack of intellectual gifts but its way of looking on other people. Fundamentalism as a movement has no insight into ways in which it might live along with Christians who think quite differently, or live alongside people who are not Christians at all. Its only real positive message to anyone is that they must be converted to Christ, which in effect means that they must become fundamentalist Christians. Justification is not by faith in Jesus Christ but by conversion to fundamentalism. Of course even quite extreme fundamentalists deny that they consider non-fundamentalists not to be real Christians but this denial is merely theoretical apologetic: it does not indicate any positive impulse towards the welcoming and acceptance of non-fundamentalist Christians as they are. Fundamentalist religion does not contain any confident positive assurance that there is some other way than the fundamentalist way that is a truly valid way to Christ. Fundamentalists may well be people of excellent good will, but in this respect they are caught in the trap of their own religious convictions: however much they seek to make allowances (which in fact is extremely seldom except when under pressure from the arguments of critics), they have no positive means of asserting, as a positive good, that Christians of liberal or catholic persuasion, who accept radical biblical criticism or pursue a critical theology, are just as much accepted within the grace of God and in faith in Jesus Christ as they themselves are. Their approach is essentially an imperialistic one, and it is no accident that its flourishing coincided with the great period of Western political imperialism: its solution to religious conflict is that others must also become fundamentalists, or at least evangelicals. On the personal level this means that the basic weakness of fundamentalism is its inability to *accept* other people for what they are. This however brings us back to the rationalist character of the fundamentalist movement: doctrines and principles are primary, people, faith, and existential attitudes are secondary.

But the doctrinal character of fundamentalism is also in large measure dictated by the social functioning of fundamentalist society. It is the society, and not either the individual or the doctrinal theory, that carries out the practical evangelism. It is the life and the example of the fundamentalist society that attract the new convert; similarly, it is the pressure of life in that society that changes his new faith from a bright trust in his Lord into a deadening conformity to the norms and orthodoxies of the group. Many of the characteristics of fundamentalist society do not stem from pure doctrine but from what seem to be practical considerations. On a purely doctrinal level, for instance, some sort of minor recognition of critical study of the Bible seems possible even in highly conservative quarters; on the practical level, however, when one considers how an average fundamentalist group behaves, any such recognition or concession seems to disturb the life and activity of the group and make it more vague, its outlines more uncertain. Such practical considerations support the rigidity of the fundamentalist positions.

This applies, we may note, more to the more modern, and mainly Anglo-Saxon, evangelical fundamentalism, and less to the conservatism of the churches which derive from the older continental orthodoxies. These latter communities may enclose within themselves many of the same views as fundamentalists hold, about the Bible and about traditional doctrine; but their social stance is more related to a national church, or an ethnically-defined church, and the doctrine and ethics of that church, much less to a fundamentalist stratum existing within several churches but actually living by its own inner norms, with its own discipline, habits, ethos, literature and traditions of interpretation.

It is time, however, to return to the crucial matter of biblical interpretation. Here again my book marked, I believe, a contrast with what has generally been said by critics of fundamentalism. It is often said that fundamentalists are 'people who take the Bible literally'. This however is a mistake. Fundamentalist interpretation concentrates not on taking the Bible literally, but on taking it so that it will appear to have been inerrant, without error in point of fact. Far from insisting that interpretation should be literal, it veers back and forward between the literal sense and a non-literal sense, in order to preserve the impression that the Bible is, especially in historical regards, always 'right'. For instance, many or most fundamentalists do not maintain that the world was created in seven days: rather, they think that it came to be in a long process, lasting perhaps millions of years, and, in order to make room for this 'true' account, they 'stretch out' the Genesis narrative (the so-called 'gap theory'), abandoning its literal meaning and extending it to make it fit the facts which they – from a slight influence of modern scientific knowledge – accept as true. Any literal interpretation would have to say that the Bible – or more correctly this particular chapter of the Bible – held the world to have been created in seven days, with the corollary that the story is legendary or mythical, and this is of course the right way in which to take it. Fundamentalist interpretation, in some highly influential currents, abandons the literal interpretation in order to secure one that seems to make the text inerrant. It is the inerrancy of the Bible, especially its truth in historical regards, that is the fundamentalist position, and not the notion that it must always be interpreted literally. The contrary is the case. It is the *critical* interpretation of the Bible that has noticed, and given full value to, the literal sense. In this sense, as Ebeling and others have noted, the critical movement is the true heir of the Reformation with its emphasis on the plain sense of scripture. It is precisely because of its respect for the literal sense that critical scholarship has concluded that different sources in (say) the Pentateuch, or the gospels, must be identified. For instance, if one takes the Genesis story literally, Ishmael was a small child when Hagar was driven into the wilderness: Abraham 'put him on her shoulder' (21.14), and later, when she was exhausted, she 'threw' the child under a bush (v. 15). Gen. 17.25 however says that Ishmael was already thirteen years old before Isaac was born. The observation of hundreds of such minor discrepancies, patiently pieced together over a long period, led to the critical reconstruction, i.e. the suggestion that the genealogical material of Gen. 17 (P?) was written independently of the personal story about Hagar and does not fit with it in this respect. Only the recognition of the source division can do justice to what is actually said in the passages concerned. Characteristic conservative treatments, as I have shown, depart from the natural meaning of the texts in order to force upon them an apologetically-motivated harmonization which will evade the fact of the contradiction.

Thus I should make clear the basic direction of my own

criticism of fundamentalism. My argument is not, as some liberal or radical opinion would have it, that scripture cannot really be authority over the church. Nor do I suggest that the real problems of theology and doctrine lie in the world of modern thought, so that they cannot be decided by ancient scripture. This may or may not be so, but it is not part of my thesis. My argument is simply and squarely that fundamentalist interpretation, because it insists that the Bible cannot err, not even in historical regards, has been forced to interpret the Bible wrongly; conversely, it is the critical analysis, and not the fundamentalist approach, that has taken the Bible for what it is and interpreted it accordingly. The problem of fundamentalism is that, far from being a biblical religion, an interpretation of scripture in its own terms, it has evaded the natural and literal sense of the Bible in order to imprison it within a particular tradition of human interpretation. The fact that this tradition – one drawn from older Protestant orthodoxy – assigns an extremely high place to the nature and authority of the Bible in no way alters the situation described, namely that it functions as a human tradition which obscures and imprisons the meaning of scripture.

To say this is not to suggest that there are no good things to be found in fundamentalist society and its conceptions of scripture and religion. There are indeed good things – these good things, however, all end up by being spoiled, spoiled by the inability of the movement to show any real acceptance of other Christians or of non-Christians, spoiled by the suspicion and lack of freedom that its own exclusiveness engenders, and spoiled by the rationalistic mind-set into which it is led by its own doctrine of scripture.

Since we have come back to the rationalism of fundamentalist Christianity, it may be helpful to offer a further illustration. For mainstream Christianity in most of its forms a scriptural passage functions as part of the relation of faith in Jesus Christ. The passage calls for faith and is effective because the understanding of the passage is part of the question of faith in him. In fundamentalism the *general* principle of the inerrancy or infallibility of scripture obviates this relation: once it is known that in principle all that is in scripture is true, it then rationally follows that all its detailed statements are true. Conversely, if any detailed statement is in any way wrong, it rationally follows that the whole is undependable. In fundamentalism the Christian's handling of biblical materials thus becomes a *rational* deduction from the already accepted principle of infallibility.

This is well evidenced by the so-called 'domino theory', very manifest in fundamentalist thinking. The argument goes thus: if any point in scripture becomes uncertain, then that makes another uncertain, and that overturns yet another, and in the end no one will have any assurance about anything that is based upon scripture. Faith in Jesus Christ will thus be gone. This argument does not depend on faith; on the contrary, it displays the absence of faith. It depends on a rational nexus. If in fact one's faith is in a person, in Jesus Christ, and if one knows that person as a person, then that faith is not going to be overturned by any changes in the meaning or certainty of one part of scripture or another. When people worry that doubts about this part or that of scripture will destroy their faith, they make it evident that they do not really live by faith.

Consider also this further point. When one examines fundamentalism, not from the aspect of doctrine or of theory, but from the experience of talking with actual fundamentalists, nothing is more striking than the unusual power exercised within fundamentalist Christianity by *human authority*. The outsider, talking with fundamentalists, might imagine that he would be constantly invited to comment on scriptural passages and say what he thinks they mean. Not at all. What fundamentalists characteristically talk about in conversation is their own leaders. One cannot talk for ten seconds before the name of the first of them comes up. And he leads on to a second, and he to a third. What about the doctrine of John Stott? What about the scholarship of this or that other? The constant appeal to this series of *gurus*, and not to scripture itself, is one of the most striking features of modern fundamentalist thinking. The prominence of these *gurus* in fundamentalism is far greater than the prominence of biblical scholars or theologians in non-fundamentalist Christianity; their authority in ideological matters is far greater than that of mere bishops, moderators and church leaders within denominations. These ideological leaders are quoted and requoted not so much for what they are in themselves – the average fundamentalist may have read little of their works and may thoroughly misunderstand what they actually think, as pointed out above – but because they are supposed to be a support to the popular fundamentalist ideology. Here again we have a position, supposedly founded upon the divine authority of scripture, actually producing a situation in which human ideological authority is much stronger than in the average current of mainstream Christianity.

This may lead us suitably to a further question, namely, how far we can detect change for the better in the total fundamentalist/conservative evangelical society. One of the chief arguments made in criticism of my book by conservative reviewers has been the argument that, even if things were in the past as I have described, they are no longer so in the present: the books I used, the sources I quoted, lie in the past, but in present-day fact many of these phenomena no longer are so and fundamentalism has a much more pleasant face than I have suggested.

Let me therefore introduce an autobiographical aspect, which will help to illustrate and make clear the angle from which I view the development of fundamentalism, at least in our English-speaking Christianity. I was of course never a highly historical-critical scholar, very much the reverse: my most important books have been in certain senses devoted to an attempt to overcome unfortunate applications of supposedly historical method. When my most important book, *The Semantics of Biblical Language*, was published, it was greeted with excessive favour by many conservatives because it showed a way around the arguments of the then 'biblical theology' which was pressing them quite hard. I know the evangelical world well from my student days, when I was active in an evangelical organization, the Edinburgh University Christian Union. This was not a movement in which liberal thinking and biblical criticism were welcome – far from it. No one within it used these lines of thought more than minimally or talked positively of them. Nevertheless conservatism, as modern conservative evangelicalism and fundamentalism represent it, was not the keynote of the movement. Its keynote was not biblical inerrancy or infallibility but the centrality of the *doctrinal substance* of the Bible. What was talked about was the doctrine of the Pauline letters, of St John, of the other gospels. Basic to the movement was the primacy of faith and the refusal to adopt an apologetic attitude which could 'prove' the reliability of biblical materials; along with this went the emphasis on personal, existential relations. One refused to spend time arguing about the numbers of the Israelites on their march from Egypt to Canaan, or even about the 'reliability' of the 'evidence' for the resurrection. The doctrinal centre, and not the historical margin, of the Bible was emphasized. Precisely because of this position, this was a very powerful and effective evangelistic agency with a profound outreach and impact. If this had still been the state of the conservative evangelical movement I would never have thought of writing my book *Fundamentalism*.

What I did observe, when many years later I came back to study the phenomenon, was that almost all that had made my own experience of evangelicalism tolerable, creative and enjoyable had been cut away. The insights that had come from existentialism and Barthianism had been quite suppressed: modern conservative evangelicalism is almost as if these movements had never existed. The emphasis on a traditional rational orthodoxy has completely triumphed over them. The much-vaunted improvement in learning and scholarship, on which conservatives so greatly pride themselves, only highlights the steady and emphatic rejection by evangelical leadership, as expressed in the scholarly literature, of those elements which I would say are truly evangelical and which make evangelicalism creative and viable, and their insistence on the necessity of those which are most unevangelical: in particular, the emphasis on the historical inerrancy of scripture, and the concomitant embracing of a rationalist-apologetic-historicist approach for the defence of this essential point. It was the reading of the scholarly literature of modern conservative evangelicism that deeply appalled me and set the tone of much that I wrote in *Fundamentalism*. The earlier drafts I wrote were more kind towards the movement; it was my increasing reading in the current literature, the literature, shall we say, from the fifties to the present day, that increasingly determined my mind against this movement.

Let us again put it in this way: evangelicalism as a movement has a choice before it between two leading principles. One is that of personal religion with the primacy of faith; the other is that of orthodoxy reinforced by rationalist argumentation. To me the heart of evangelical religion lies in the former; fundamentalism, seeking to defend the evangelical tradition, ends by losing the very centre of it. The fact that I use this argument should, incidentally, dispose of the idea that my general position is an anti-evangelical one: as I have made plain throughout, it is only by making a clear abandonment of the fundamentalist/conservative position that a true evangelical position can be maintained.

Anyway, at this point I am simply trying to explain how it

seemed to me, as I studied the subject, that the situation in fundamentalism (and/or conservative evangelicalism), measured by its grasp on the basic Christian verities, had greatly deteriorated in the last decades. Conservative apologists see it the other way: they paint a picture of a movement that has in every way improved, where everything is getting better and better. Now I would be happy to admit that in certain segments it is getting better and better: I only want to make it clear that it is getting worse as well. I find the understanding of scripture in the mind of the fundamentalist student of 1979 not more open and enlightened than it was thirty or forty years ago, but often more primitive, closed and backward-looking than it was then. If on the one side we have to note the learning that can appear in modern fundamentalist scholarship, on the other side we have to take notice of the corresponding dark side, for instance the remarkable influence exercised in the last decade or so by a phoney pseudo-intellectual like Francis Schaeffer. On the scene of the world church, we have witnessed in the very last years the use of manifest ecclesiastical power politics to achieve a fundamentalist take-over in the large Concordia Seminary, as already mentioned, and a similar attempt is reported as now under way among the Southern Baptists. Things of this kind are forgotten by those who paint for us the bright picture of a new advanced and open conservatism, free from the stains of the older fundamentalism. In many ways the older fundamentalism was better and more honest. The increasing influence of evangelicalism of all sorts in the last decade or so has worked at both ends of the scale: if at one end it has worked for a greater freedom and openness, at the other end it has functioned to deepen the bonds of the most intransigent fundamentalism.

This argument about change has a deeper dimension. Conservative apologists have been quick to say that the books I read, the people I quoted, are people of the past. Things, they say, are changing very rapidly. Books that were published six or eight years ago (!) are no longer representative of opinion. Schaeffer, whom I just mentioned, was (I have been told) influential about eight years ago but is no longer so. This is indeed a high rate of change.

This argument, however, cannot be taken seriously. The books that I quoted are the books that are standard conservative evangelical reading *now*, the leaders that I quoted are the leaders *now* – or, if they were discussed as leaders of an earlier stage in the movement, they were leaders of a stage that led up to what we have now. The image of a conservative evangelicalism that is changing so fast that books written six or eight years ago are already out of date is surely a ludicrous one. This is a *conservative* movement and rightly claims to be such. 'Conservative' can only mean that it retains strong continuity with its past, with its own older traditions. A movement where books written six or eight years ago are already out of date is a movement that is travelling very fast. Liberal theology in its most lively days never made progress at anything like this rate. Conservatism in a movement can be a justified thing, but it must mean that a movement accepts responsibility for its own past, for the traditions out of which it came. And this means that those 'conservative evangelicals' who are so anxious to disown the term 'fundamentalist' and to deny their own fundamentalist intellectual past tradition are not doing anything very admirable. For, as I have said, fundamentalism has its good sides and in its history took some decisions that can be defended as right. To disavow the designation 'fundamentalist' and prefer the term 'conservative evangelical' is not, as many think, to escape from the unpleasant associations of the former word: on the contrary, the latter is in many ways a more shameful self-designation, for it betrays the belief that conservatism is the basic criterion for truth in religion and the will that the gospel should be bound to this human ideology. Fundamentalist and conservative apologists, when they attempt to insist on the doctrinal position of the very last moment, so that books even six years old can be regarded as out of date, seem to be denying the validity of their own history, denying the past out of which they have come; they insist that the outsider should not look at that past, as clear documents manifest it, but listen solely to what is said today by the present spokesmen of the conservative viewpoint. The similarities between fundamentalist Protestantism and traditional Roman Catholicism have often been remarked; one of them, the prominent place of human authority, has already been noticed in this paper. Again, the fundamentalist doctrine of biblical infallibility has a marked analogy with the doctrine of papal infallibility which was promulgated at about the same time; and, if this is so, the modern fundamentalist spokesman who wants nothing to be heard but the voice of the fundamentalist you are at present speaking to is taking a position rather

like that of Pius IX in the (doubtless apocryphal) saying attribu-
ted to him: *La tradizione sono io,* 'It is I who am the tradition.'

Fundamentalism is one of those phenomena that will always
and necessarily seem quite different to those who are within it
and to those who are outside it. This has just to be accepted as
a fact: any statement about fundamentalism, made from outside, will commonly be perceived by fundamentalists as a mis-
description and discounted as such, unless it can be utilized for
the support and profit of their own position, as statements
made from outside sometimes can. This will not change much.
And of course fundamentalists are entitled to think about their
own religion as they like. What they do not have the right to
do is to claim that their own understanding of their own ideology, as seen from within, has any sort of priority over other
people's understanding of fundamentalism, as it is seen from
without. Active fundamentalists are quick to decry as misdes-
cription any critical account of their own position: persons
emerging from fundamentalism, and those who have known it
and abandoned it, see things differently. Fundamentalism,
however, forms a powerful, unitary, integral propagandist
centre: by contrast, the voices of its critics are dispersed and
they do not have a unitary viewpoint or a united message to
put forward. This is a reason why careful and penetrating study
of the subject has to be carried on. Scholars commonly imply a
rejection of fundamentalism, often they look on it with discom-
fort and ridicule, but not so often do they really *study* it. There
is a need for a body of careful analysis of fundamentalism in its
impact on biblical study and theology, made from outside, to
set against the accounts, invariably propagandistic, which fundamentalists give of their own thinking and operations.

It is not always to be supposed, however, that fundamentalism in its actual operation is a doctrinally strict movement. As
an ideology it is strict and narrow, and it may be that within
evangelicalism today it forms the only block of strictly applied
doctrine. But exceptions are made for anything that seems to
be of profit to the total cause of evangelicalism. When one looks
at the larger scene of evangelicalism, as it has recently developed in a country like England, one receives the impression
that the actual criterion for acceptance is not doctrinal or scriptural but political (in the sense not of national politics but of
church politics and partisan identity). By 'political' I mean
adherence to and support for the various evangelical causes and

organizations, and above all willingness to let oneself be identified as an aspirant to the evangelical identity. Books have
begun to appear, claiming to have been written by 'conservative
evangelicals', which made wide forays in pursuit of the 'New
Hermeneutic' and other such theological fashions.[5] But of
course no work that welcomes the 'New Hermeneutic' can be
regarded as sincerely *conservative*, for this hermeneutic, as its
name implies, is a quite untried modern innovation and exactly
the sort of thing that conservatism exists to prevent. Perhaps of
course the evangelical authors have simply misunderstood the
presuppositions within critical theology and philosophical tradition upon which the 'New Hermeneutic' rests; but clearly a
movement that admits the 'New Hermeneutic' has abandoned
all right to count as a barrier against theological innovation, and
one might as well admit *The Myth of God Incarnate* and be done
with it. What would Warfield have said of the 'New Hermeneutic'? Why then does this quite modern theological innovation receive some degree of acceptance within a movement
where fundamentalism remains the dominant ideology? What
happens is that, if a scholar or writer associates with the evangelical movements, writes for their periodicals, allows his name
to be used by them, and avoids actively disturbing fundamentalist opinion, he will be accepted, even if he shows an interest
in dubious things like form criticism or in grossly non-conservative trends like the 'New Hermeneutic'. The criterion is parti-
sanship in acceptance of the evangelical identity. This again is
one of the ways in which human authority lies at the base of
the whole matter, the authority of the community for which
evangelical identity is the essence of its own self-consciousness.

It may be thought, finally, that this lecture is lacking in one
thing, namely, that it is lacking in any sense of the weaknesses
and defects of critical scholarship as applied to the Bible. Several
critics of my own book have remarked that I seemed to be
totally satisfied with the perfections of the critical approach.
And it is true that I did not say anything along this line in my
book, leaving this point as a friendly little trap into which
several duly fell.[6] For of course I am quite ready to agree that
some quite impressive, even if not decisive, arguments can be
directed against the finality of the critical approach to the Bible.
One can, for instance, urge that it is lacking in spiritual relevance and inspirational value; and one can urge that it is historicist and unable to escape from a purely historical dimension.

I have myself just written an introduction for a little book by Professor Stuhlmacher which makes some such criticisms along with other points.[7] But these criticisms, however far they may be right or wrong, do not come into the discussion with fundamentalism for a simple reason: even if these arguments against a critical reading of scripture are valid, they are even more valid as against the conservative biblical scholarship revered and accepted by fundamentalist apologists. No one is going to be inspired or spiritually enriched by learning from a conservative commentary that St Paul did after all write the letters to Timothy and Titus. No one is going to go forth to evangelize the world simply on the ground that a fundamentalist scholar has proved to his satisfaction that the Paul of Acts is in absolute agreement with the Paul of the Epistles. In fact nothing is more stodgy, dull, uninspiring and lacking in fervour than the fundamentalist scholarship of our time. For spirituality and inspiration von Rad and Bultmann lie far ahead at every point. What conservative scholarship supplies, and what it is valued for, is not inspiration or spirituality, it is the rehearsal of and reinforcement of the ideology of *conservatism*.

The same is the case with historicism. It is possible to put up a good case against historicism, though it is by no means clear that most biblical criticism has been historicist in any case. And fundamentalist apologists do sometimes attack historicism, thinking that they thereby do some damage to biblical criticism. But this is on the theoretical level only. In its actual scholarly production conservative scholarship for the most part accepts the methods of historicism more fully than critical scholarship has ever done. Far from repudiating the false values of historicism, the scholars whom fundamentalists revere have often submitted entirely to them and argue fully within them, concealing the ideological insistence on scriptural inerrancy which dictates the actual results they derive. Kitchen's Moses who wrote the Pentateuch is very much more fully a historicist construction than are Wellhausen's sources of the Pentateuch or Noth's tradition history. In fact the acceptance of historicist method and stodgy pedantry by fundamentalists has been complete, so long as it could lead to *conservative* results. All along the line it is modern scholarship, enlivened by critical ideas, that has given the lead in the move to avoid the weaknesses of historicism; central currents of fundamentalist scholarship are still securely tied to these weaknesses. Where conservatives

have begun to look for a way out from historicism, they have
had to leave the resources of their own conservative tradition
and borrow ideas from other currents of modern theology. But
the fact and the implications of this borrowing are seldom made
clear.

If we ask what is to be done, here are some suggestions. First
of all, we should avoid thinking in terms of a scale, with extreme
fundamentalism at one end, then more moderate fundamentalism, then what we might call conservative evangelicalism, then
a variety of more liberal positions, still evangelical but gradually
becoming more liberal. Conversation shows that fundamentalists themselves commonly have a picture of this kind. They
think that we will be pleased if they only move a little bit to the
left along the scale, or if they can show that they are not so far
to the right on it as had been supposed. I don't think this
matters; in terms of value there is little difference. The extreme
fundamentalist has a certain logic on his side and has certain
advantages that the modern 'conservative evangelical' does not
have; his position is commonly a more honest one, and also it
is upon his ideology that the more moderate really lean. But on
the other hand the extreme fundamentalist position is increasingly untenable in the modern world. Minor movements along
this scale are, in any case, of little importance; they are usually
made with the intention of keeping as much as possible of
traditional extreme fundamentalism, while getting rid of some
of the sheer absurdities that attach to it. I think we have to be
clear that minor adjustments are of no real importance and that
we must get rid of the whole thing, that is, that the entire
apparatus of fundamentalist belief about scripture has to be
dismantled, and that we have to be clear that we are doing this,
and why.

How, however, is this to be done? Firstly, we have to build
a doctrine of scripture 'from below' and not 'from above': we
should read it for what it itself is and what it itself says, and
avoid reading into it 'the evangelical doctrine of scripture', i.e.
the opinions that some people in evangelical Protestantism held
about the Bible two centuries or so ago. We should be clear
from the beginning that at least historically scripture is errant
and fallible, or more correctly that historical accuracy or infallibility is not a concern of scripture itself at all, but is rather
something imported from Protestant tradition and imposed
upon scripture. We should recognize the likely presence of

different sources, of pseudonymity, or of derivation of material from long lasting previous stages, and so on. The recognition of these is not a concession or an acceptance of an occasional weakness but something to be gladly and confidently proclaimed as an essential means of insight into the nature of scripture itself.

Secondly, on the other hand, actual critical procedures and results are a different matter: there should be no idea of forcing these upon fundamentalists or upon anyone else. They are only means by which we read and appreciate the meaning of scripture. Theologically, they do not belong to the substance of Christian faith, and from a scholarly point of view they are always subject to revision, correction and if necessary replacement by a new position. Fundamentalists do not have to be asked to *accept* such things as the documents of the Pentateuch or the probable non-historicity of much that is in the Fourth Gospel. All that is required is the acceptance that these things are *possible* and that they are *legitimate* for use in the church and in the teaching of scripture.

Beyond this there lies, however, the practical problem of the social and organizational structure of fundamentalism, its network of societies, institutions, colleges, periodicals, newspapers, research centres and so on. All of this is organized so as to provide the maximum resistance to the entry of any non-evangelical and non-fundamentalist opinion. Such opinions are admitted, so far as possible, only when filtered through the interpretation of more or less ideologically sound conservative spokesmen. This is the way in which this society works and always has worked. The problem cannot be approached creatively through legal and institutional power, which is exactly the channel that conservatism has so often used. The most promising avenue is that of increased intellectual exposure: that is, increased study, from outside the fundamentalist society and its network, of its operations, its publications, and its ways of thinking. Until now the very obscurity of fundamentalist operations, the humble and poor-quality character of the publications, the unsophisticated and uncomprehending obscurantism of its relation to the world of theology, have actually been a force that protected the fundamentalist movement from the critical gaze that it deserved to have directed upon it, and thus enabled it to continue all the more steadily on its course.[8] It is to be expected that this will alter in the years to come. The purpose of such intellectual exposure is not to induce the fundamentalist to change his mind: as far as I am concerned, he may stay as he is if he likes. But it will make a difference to his environment. It will make a difference to all those who are under pressure from the arguments of fundamentalists, and to all those who are or have been within fundamentalism but are seeking to find their way out. In the long run it is not the fundamentalist's picture of himself, but the outside world's picture of him, that matters. And the intellectual respectability, which the fundamentalist so fervently covets, may become rather harder to attain. The world may thus become somewhat more difficult for fundamentalism to succeed in. And for evangelicals in particular this may mean the increasing need to develop a theological position that is not a mild deviation from the fundamentalist ideology but a real and radical alternative.

6

The Bible as a Political Document

This lecture is not a work of exact biblical scholarship: it will not seek to prove, with precise exegetical detail, what the Bible had to say about politics. Nor is it a work of positive and constructive theology, seeking to declare what the message of the Bible for political life may be. Nor, again, is it a work of exact historical scholarship – for which the lecturer, needless to say, would be very ill qualified – that would endeavour to survey what the political effects and the political impact of the Bible throughout history have been. My purpose is much more inexact and impressionistic. I want to isolate and identify a variety of political images that the Bible seems, at various times and in the eyes of various societies, to have projected, images of social and political organization therefore that have seemed to people, rightly or wrongly, to have derived from the Bible or at least to be consonant with the Bible; and, in relation to each of these images, I want to consider from what stratum of biblical thinking it derives and to what extent, if any, it is justified when seen against the actual intentions of that particular stratum of the Bible. For, as I have already implied, the Bible does not project one unitary political image or message, but several different images and messages are, at least *prima facie*, derivable from it. And therefore it may seem worth while to look at the diversity of these images. In this sense I am seeking, not to validate any image or message by precise exegetical confirmation, but to construct a rather loose or vague typology of such images, which may then enable us to classify and interpret the diversity of the political effects which the Bible seems to have exercised.

The question might well be asked why I am doing this at all, and the answer to this question will help to launch us into our investigation. I pose the question of the Bible as a political document because of my special interests as an Old Testament scholar. For, as I shall show, the Old Testament has often been the primary source, often much more important than the New Testament, for those who have tried to find a basis for political ideas in the Bible. Let us take an example straight away: of all the large-scale social effects exercised by the Bible, none has been more striking than the prohibition of the lending of money at interest. This was standard church doctrine for many centuries over large areas, even if that doctrine was never fully effective in practice. Now the prohibition of lending at interest could not well be based upon the New Testament: on the contrary, one might say, Jesus rather encouraged the practice, for he is said to have reproved the man who, given a sum of money to keep by his master, wrapped it in a napkin or dug a hole and kept it in the ground. 'You ought to have invested my money with the bankers, and at my coming I should have received what was my own *with interest*' (Matt. 25.27). Only a parable, of course; but even a parable puts in a certain light the practices that it uses as an image of reality: we can hardly imagine Jesus saying this if the earning of interest on capital had been for him a matter of intrinsic evil. So, if one was against the taking of interest on loans, it was of little use to appeal to the teaching of Jesus. In fact, in so far as people looked to the Bible for guidance in this regard,[1] they looked to the Old Testament, and there, it was understood, the laws of Exodus, Leviticus and Deuteronomy forbade the exaction of interest by Jews from debtors who were also Jews. 'To a foreigner you may lend upon interest; but to your brother you shall not lend upon interest' (Deut. 23.20). And upon an exegetical basis in laws of this kind Christian Europe over some centuries sought to build a society in which the levying of interest was forbidden – a course that, paradoxically, did a great deal of good to the Jews, for the laws were so interpreted as to mean that, within Christendom, Christians could not exact interest from other Christians but Jews could do so, and this gave a livelihood to many Jews in a society in which they might otherwise have been left without means of sustenance.

This then was one of the images that the Bible cast into the soul of medieval Europe. But, we are entitled to ask, how was it in fact an ancient Israel? Was it really a society in which credit

could be obtained without the payment of interest? If so, what
a paradise for debtors, and how different from our own civilization, where we groan under our hire purchase and our mortgage repayments! Can it really have been so? Mesopotamian
sources of comparable epochs show us a society in which the
supply of credit was highly organized, and rates of interest
were high, often twenty or thirty per cent, sometimes reaching
up to fifty or sixty, a figure that even the modern world can
scarcely emulate. Such figures may seem high, but think of the
risk to the lender: a bad harvest, a plague of locusts, a fire, a
nocturnal disappearance of the debtor across the borders into
Gaza or Phoenicia, all of them a much greater risk in a time
when there were no police, no passports, virtually no state
services – and the creditor would have lost not only his interest,
but his principal as well. It would seem only reasonable that
the lender should receive some compensation both for the use
of his money and for the attendant risk, and ancient Israel must
have been a strange sort of society if it refused entirely to
recognize this.

In fact, however, it was probably not so in Israel, and there
were arrangements for the supply of credit on interest that not
only existed but were recognized and recommended by the law.
A probable example is the law of the Hebrew slave (Ex. 21.2–
6). A man might 'buy' a Hebrew slave, who would work for six
years and then go free: behind this there may lie a complete
system combining elements of credit, interest and poor relief.
It may be that a man in need might sell himself into slavery,
perhaps with his wife and family, and during that time the
produce of their labour went to their owner, and that produce
formed his interest; but the law regulated the matter and
insisted that, at the end of six years, whether or not such a man
had repaid his debt, he must go free.[2] Paradoxically, medieval
Christendom, in its efforts to evade or to get around what it
understood to be the provisions of the Pentateuchal law, may
have stumbled upon forms of contract, through temporary sale,
antichresis and the like, which came close to the actuality of
Israelite practice. If this is so, then Israel did not prohibit all
interest on credit but confined it to certain types that were
socially and religiously acceptable. When we read that 'usury'
or 'interest' are totally forbidden, this may probably refer to
certain kinds of simple money loan which, when granted to the
man who is already impoverished, tend to reduce him – as is

still the case today – to even more desperate destitution than that in which he began.

I do not wish, however, to pursue this matter in greater detail: I cite it only as an illustration. It shows us, first of all, how the political and social impact of the Bible has often come from the Old Testament rather than from the New, and, secondly, how the political image, *understood* to be cast by the Bible, may be a very substantial misunderstanding of the actuality of what was going on in biblical times. These are two points that will recur in our further discussion.

Rather than spend more time in preamble, I propose to launch out into the first of the biblical images I want to talk about, and it is what I would call the *theocratic image*. According to the theocratic image God has laid down the way in which society ought to be governed and its affairs conducted. The essential constitution for human society has been written by God. These are not human regulations worked out by people who thought that such and such was the best thing for society, these are explicit divine regulations. They establish a centre of authority, in a person like Moses or the kings of Israel and Judah; around him they range, however vaguely as seen from today's point of view, various elders, ministers, judges and military commanders; and alongside this they lay down all sorts of particular enactments: what is to be done if a man is killed, whether accidentally or intentionally, what is to be done if a man has no son to whom to leave his inheritance but a family of daughters only (Num. 27, the story of the daughters of Zelophehad), and what is the rule in a polygamous society if a man has two wives and prefers one of them but his firstborn is the son of the one he does not like (Deut. 21. 15–17). Much of this material has the form of laws but not all of it is so: the theocratic norms are enforced as often through narratives as through laws. Narratives tell how the great ones behaved, what they demanded, what they counted as right and necessary. From all of this there came the picture of a society where things were what they were because the basic norms and structures were directly laid down by God. He laid down the degrees within which marriage was permitted, just as he laid down which birds or animals might be eaten, or what should be done if a dead body was found in the fields of a city, with no clues to the cause or culprit, or even what procedure should be followed if a man became suspicious of the doings of his wife and wanted to know if she had been guilty of adulterous conduct (Num. 5). All such material has gone to form or to support the theocratic image cast by the Bible.

Now Christendom never accepted all these regulations in detail: many of them were deemed to belong to the past stage of Judaism and not to the newer world of Christianity. But this did not alter the fact that these elements continued within Christianity to support a theocratic image. Though Christendom was not ancient Jewry, it was a society theocratically ordained: God had laid down the rules, and the authorities, in enforcing these rules, had to understand that it was no mere human ordinances, but the divine prescription for society, that they were enforcing. From this root comes all that social apparatus that is commonly called the establishment of religion: the coronation service, the linkage of church and state, the table of forbidden degrees for marriage, and part of the way in which crimes against person and property have been regarded, so also (in part) the way in which the status of women and the possibilities of divorce and abortion have been understood in Christian societies until very recently. Under the theocratic image of society all these things were laid down: one of the main functions of the church, as men of the state saw it, was to tell everyone that this was so.

If we go back, however, into the Old Testament itself, and ask what were the sources and epochs from which this theocratic image came, we find rather ambiguous answers. The most positively theocratic material comes, according to a probable analysis, from a later period (I take the Pentateuchal stratum commonly designated as P as the model for the theocratic image as it is developed here). If this is right, it was during the Persian Empire, when the Jews had lost their independence except for minor local affairs, and when they were a rather small local community governed by a priestly aristocracy, that their theocratic texts reached their fullest development. This fitted, indeed, a society with a priestly leadership, acknowledging the priestly norms as the norms of the society because they came from God himself. But, if it fitted, it fitted because beyond it there lay another and a quite different power, the power of the Persian emperor, whose norms and principles were quite different from those of the Jewish community and derived not from the God of Israel but from Ahura Mazda. And for later Christendom, much as it supported itself upon the theocratic image of the Bible, there was one difficulty. In Christendom, up to the French and American revolutions, theocracy meant more than any other single thing the legitimacy of monarchy, what at its highest level was defined as the Divine Right of Kings. But about kings and monarchy the Old Testament itself was equivocal. Its theocracy was, in the later portions, a priestly theocracy; the secular prince was there but only with very circumscribed functions. In the older history of Israel and Judah there were indeed kings, and the kings contributed much to the theocratic image, but the stories themselves made it clear that the origin of the monarchy was theologically ambivalent. This was not a society which had begun, as certain Mesopotamian societies had begun, 'when kingship was lowered from heaven': no, kingship was not lowered from heaven in the beginning, on the contrary there had been a long time in Israel before kingship began, and when it began it began not as an element in the theocracy but as a rebellion against it. When the people went to Samuel and demanded, 'Give us a king to govern us,' Samuel prayed to the Lord, and he said, 'They have not rejected you, but they have rejected me from being king over them' (I Sam. 8.6f.). The idea of having a human king was a revolt against God. In respect of human monarchy the theocracy was thus ambiguous. But in most of traditional Christianity this ambiguity was suppressed. The alternative, republicanism or democracy, some sort of system under which institutions derived from the people, seemed even less well supported by Holy Writ: after all, in so far as monarchy was to be faulted as a revolt against God, it was so exactly because the people had demanded it, it was they who were to blame. Anyway, as people perceived it, the theocratic image enabled them to see society as a hierarchical organism under a divinely instituted human leadership, rightly and soundly constituted because God had made it so. In this respect the theocratic image derived from the Bible fused with ideas of power and authority, the source of which lay above all in the Roman Empire. In this sense the theocratic image supports ordained authority, or at least it does so most of the time.

For a contrast to the theocratic image I shall turn rather to the New Testament. As I have said, those who seek a biblical basis for their political ideas have often, even if unconsciously, turned primarily to the Old Testament, and one reason for this has been that the New Testament, on so many burning social and political issues, seemed either to say nothing or to take an embarrassingly neutral stance. In this respect Jesus of Nazareth must be judged to have been rather neglectful. On the essential question, for example, of whether we should have a socialist or a free-enterprise economy, he said nothing at all. Perhaps he thought that the question came under the head of his guidance given to the man who came saying, 'Master, bid my brother divide the inheritance with me' (Luke 12.13). The passage continues: 'But he said unto him, "Man, who made me a judge or a divider over you?" ' – which seems to mean that there are certain human struggles and disagreements which God, or Jesus, does not intend to settle: such things are human business, and there is no divine directive or initiative intended to regulate them. There is indeed a law of God, or an instruction of Jesus, which has to be borne in mind, and obeyed, in such matters: 'Take heed, and beware of all covetousness: for a man's life does not consist in the abundance of his possessions.' But this necessarily means that the divine theocracy does not settle every human question. And this is in accord with the more famous answer of Jesus to the question about the tribute money: 'Render to Caesar the things that are Caesar's, and to God the things that are God's' (Mark 12.17; Matt. 22.21; Luke 20.25). Obviously the answer leaves one enormous gap: it does not tell us what is Caesar's and what is God's; but in principle it makes one striking point, which differs in essence from the theocratic image: there is at least something, somewhere, that is Caesar's, not everything is God's. There is authority on earth that is not directly validated by the Jewish theocratic image. There is thus a certain dualism in society: not everything can be derived from one sole principle. And thus, to the disgust of radicals and committed conservatives alike, and of all those who consider that political involvement is the essence of Christianity, Jesus seems in some situations to have taken a position of some neutrality and refused to align God in the partisan struggles of men. Those bishops and church leaders who have sought, rightly or wrongly, to keep the church separate from party political struggles have been following in this tradition. A certain neutralism on Jesus' part, towards at least some human squabbles, partisanships and conflicts seems to be a genuine part of the biblical inheritance.

Now, when I use the word 'Jesus' in this connection, I mean Jesus as he is portrayed in the gospels as we have them. It is

necessary to say this because not all agree that the actual Jesus
thought and acted as he is there portrayed. In particular, according to one interpretation of the evidence, the real and historical
Jesus was deeply involved in the party politics of his time: far
from being above the human conflicts of the Jews in the Roman
Empire, he was an activist nationalist and revolutionary worker,
allied with the Zealot movement and seeking to promote a
military conflict with Rome. This militaristic Jesus, a sort of Che
Guevara of the time, was later covered up by the writers of the
gospels, who wanted the Roman Empire to look favourably on
Christianity and brought this about by representing Jesus as a
non-worldly and non-political man of God.[3] I am not concerned
to argue here the rights and the wrongs of this position. I
merely reiterate that Jesus *as depicted in the gospels* is not a
militaristic revolutionary of that kind; and it is from the Jesus
of the gospels, and not from the reconstructed Jesus of Zealot
sympathies, that a quite special image of the political impact of
the Bible has fallen upon later Christendom.

But, even if only negatively, the position just described helps
us to see one of the things about Jesus that was different from
the more purely theocratic image cast by some Old Testament
sources. For Jesus it was much more clear that the actual power,
even in Jewish affairs, came from Rome. As we saw, the theocratic image had its fullest expression, perhaps, in texts written
under the Persian Empire; but Persia, though it was the world
power, was relatively remote, was quite favourable to Jewish
religious needs, and was not much inclined to meddle in every-
day details. Under Persia it was possible for Jewish thinkers to
dream that they formed a small but virtually independent com-
monwealth living under the plan dictated by God. Under Rome
this was no longer so easy: Rome was close at hand, its power
reached into the detailed day-to-day life of Judaea, it seemed to
threaten Jewish religious sensibilities more fearfully, and people
were therefore more inclined to suppose, as the Zealots claimed,
that divine rule demanded the overthrow of Roman power.
This being so, it is all the more significant that the Jesus of the
gospels, and I am inclined to believe the real Jesus also, did not
align himself with this demand. Thus, alongside the more
purely theocratic image, there stands another, the image of a
world where not all is regulated by the command of God, at
least not directly, an image that recognizes as a legitimate factor
a force that derives from elsewhere.[4]

In the older Christendom the theocratic image was no doubt the dominant and most common one; in more modern times it has come to be increasingly displaced by others. Many people in different ages have thought that the church ought to address itself to the state and to society, protesting against the evils of contemporary life and calling for reform if not for revolution. Especially since the nineteenth century has this been so. As has been remarked, those who have felt this way did not always find very much clear precedent or express encouragement in the words of Jesus or in the teaching of the New Testament church: for that church, so far as we can see, did comparatively little to address itself to the task of social reform in the Roman Empire. Paul's failure to say anything substantial about slavery, when he was writing the letter to Philemon which involved that very subject, was worrying; and that same apostle's doctrine that the powers that be are ordained by God and that anyone who resists that power is resisting God and will receive damnation seems to support an unhealthy acceptance of things as they are. It was precisely this lack of strong support in the New Testament that made many Christians, anxious to work for social protest and social reform, turn to the Old Testament – a turn that was in many ways paradoxical, for the same social liberalism and reformism which in this regard turned them towards the Old Testament commonly turned them in all other regards away from it. The locus in the Old Testament which they found to be central lay in the prophets, and it has in fact become customary in the church by this time that any activity addressing the state, the social condition of the land, the political problems of the time and the like is considered to be 'prophetic' and is so named. This appeal to the prophets as the men who insisted on righteousness in the social order fitted in very well, because it coincided with a shift from one Christian perception of the Hebrew prophets to another. The older traditional Christianity had seen the prophets primarily as foretellers of the future, as predictive messianists, as men who, long before the time, told of the coming of Jesus the Christ and of his sufferings. In the newer perception of the prophets this became at best muted and indirect. A prophet, it was now said, was not a foreteller but a forthteller. He did not predict the future or, if he did so, this was not his main interest: what he did above all was to proclaim the demand of God for the realization of righteousness in social relationships here and now.

This then is our third image of the Bible's heritage in political matters, the picture of the prophet insisting on social righteousness now, a social righteousness which, it is clearly implied, the theocratic constitution of the nation has not availed to provide. The prophet is no neutral in these conflicts: he takes up the side of the weak and the oppressed, he calls for their rights, he speaks up for them before the mighty, he demands unceasingly that the will of God should be done. Unless it is done, God will not hesitate to overthrow the mighty, and the claims of a justice guaranteed by divine theocratic legitimacy, a justice that by its inaction favours the powerful and leaves the poor and the weak to suffer, will be disregarded by God himself. The prophetic image thus appeals directly to God himself: it goes over the head of the legitimate authority, saying that such legitimacy counts for nothing unless it delivers the goods in the form of social justice for all today. The prophetic image in this sense has been an important ingredient in much progressive, reformist, politically activist Christianity for the last hundred years.

When we compare it, however, with what is now known of the actual prophets of Israel, the prophetic image is also rich in paradox. The prophets were very far from being similar to the progressive, somewhat scientific, often mildly socialistic, often open-minded and generally reasonable, people who looked to them for authority and inspiration. Certainly it is true that the prophets insisted on social justice, and they were not afraid in its name to challenge the established authorities of their time. But the prophets for the most part were not reformers, and they had no new insights into the working of society to offer. Theirs was not a novel analysis, on the ground of which new perceptions of social need might arise, from which in turn demands for righteousness and mercy in new dimensions might be heard. On the contrary, in this respect the social perspectives and perceptions of the prophets were essentially conservative. What they declared was the traditional morality exacted by the God of Israel. Their message was not a new morality, but the reality of the sanctions that had been attached to the old. Take the example, typical of the early prophetic movement, of Naboth's vineyard (I Kings 21). Naboth had a vineyard, and Ahab the king wanted it, for it was near his new palace in Samaria; so he offered to buy it, or to exchange it for a better vineyard; but Naboth said, 'God forbid that I should give you the inheritance of my fathers.' When Ahab heard this, he knew there was no more he could do, for in Israel by ancient customary law it was not permitted to alienate the land that had belonged to a family. So Ahab lay down on his bed, turned his face to the wall, and would eat no bread. He did not even think of violating the customary law of his people. But Jezebel, the queen, being a foreigner, cared nothing for these things, and it took her only a moment, when she found out what had happened, to hire some false witnesses and have Naboth put out of the way. But then Elijah sought out Ahab and found him, and declared against him the judgment of God: 'Thus says the Lord, "In the place where dogs licked up the blood of Naboth, shall dogs lick your own blood." ' In all the story there is no new approach to morality: the old morality is presupposed throughout, and what the prophet insists on is the drastic character of the punishment that will follow when the old morality is transgressed.[5]

In other words, the traditional liberal and reformist perception that the system is wrong and that the system has to be changed if justice is to be made possible is lacking from the prophetic perspective. Practically never do we find the prophets putting forward any sort of practical suggestions for change in the structure of society. Jeremiah once (Jer. 34) denounces the king, Zedekiah, because he had promised release to all persons in (temporary) slavery; but this is not because Jeremiah wants to abolish the institution of such slavery, rather it is because the king, and others with him, having first promised to release these people, have gone back on their word. No impulse to reform the structure of society is to be found here. But most important in this respect is the great change of direction in the policy of the prophets that took place between Elisha and Hosea, between the ninth-century prophets and those of the eighth. In the ninth century, even if there were no plans for change in the structure of society, there were at least active prophetic interventions in political life. Clearly it was thought, in the midst of increasing Canaanization and Baalization of the land, that certain powerful circles, inclined toward fanatical, exclusive and conservative Yahwism, might be brought to power, and that such people by means of a *coup d'état* (rather than a revolution, which suggests a change of political structure or principle) might overthrow the decadent dynasty and establish a purer society under God. So Elisha anointed Jehu son of Nimshi as king over Israel and incited him to rebel and overthrow the existing government; and this he did, putting the existing king to death, having Jezebel thrown from the window, and massacring the congregation of the worshippers of Baal. Here indeed was political activism from the prophets. But the important thing is that this line was not followed further. On the contrary, when the next wave of prophetic activity began under Amos and Hosea, one of the first cardinal points in its programme was the abandonment of the line taken by Jehu: as Hosea put it (1.4) 'I will punish the house of Jehu for the blood of Jezreel' (where the great massacre had taken place). In fact from this time onwards, and throughout the main period of Hebrew prophecy, the fomenting of violent revolution and *coups d'état* is a course that the prophets abjure. It is as if they feel that the nation is too badly spoiled for the sources for its reform from within to survive: any attempt to purify through political action from within will be no purification, but only the releasing of another flow of evil. From now on, for the prophets, God will still work through political events, but not through internal political uprisings stimulated within Israel: God will act upon his people, judging and redeeming, but he will do it not through political forces from within the country, but through the power of the great empires that surround her, through Assyria, Babylonia and Persia. This particular political image, that of the God who works through political events but through those external to the nation rather than through its own internal politics, is perhaps the profoundest insight of the mature Old Testament period, at least among the prophets. It may seem at first sight surprising that it has had rather little effect on political thought, certainly much less than the image of the prophet as a pursuer of social righteousness. On further thought, however, the neglect of this insight is not so surprising. Most political ideas are concerned with the conflicts lying within one political system, while this particular biblical image cannot easily be assimilated to the internal dynamics of any particular political system.

Thus the sort of thing for which people have appealed to the prophetic image – the pressing for reform, the calling for new structures in society, the seeking of a societal pattern in which it was possible for all to live decently – all this is something that was rather little done by the actual prophets. This is not to say, however, that nothing of the kind took place. Curiously, this sort of pressure for the adjustment of society towards the greater realization of justice took place in Israel, but it was done much more through the medium of the law than through that of the prophets. The failure to perceive this may be ascribed to the long-standing Christian disposition to undervalue the law of the Old Testament and to ascribe more positive value to the prophets. On the surface the law of Israel appeared as something laid down once and for all by God through Moses, and in this sense it contributed to the theocratic image; but in fact the law was also a human social mechanism for the regulation of life, and there is plenty of evidence that it adjusted itself gradually in order to avoid the more serious injustices and the more inequitable pressures upon individuals or groups. We can see such adjustment, for instance, in the laws governing homicide. Starting from a rather primitive principle, whereby any killing counted as virtual murder and might be avenged with impunity, the law moves to the giving of sanctuary to a killer but only if it can be shown that the killing is involuntary; and from there, when the local sanctuaries came to be closed down and only the one great sanctuary at Jerusalem remained, the plan of 'cities of refuge' was set up, to provide places where the involuntary slayer might find asylum until the time came when he could again be reintegrated into society. There was thus reform in Israel, and indeed it may well have derived some of its motivation from the teaching of the prophets; but the direct means of reformist pressure came through the law rather than from the prophets.

These then are three of the great images projected by the Bible into the mind of later Christendom, the three that I have called the theocratic, the more neutral and dualistic, and the prophetic. These however, by no means exhaust the series of political images which the Bible has produced. I shall discuss more briefly another three. Our fourth image we may call the image of the migrating nation. Migration, change of location, displacement, is an image deeply burned into the soul of biblical man. The Old Testament tells of at least three major such migrations: that of Abraham, who was called by God to leave Mesopotamia and go to another country; then the great journey of the children of Israel, forty years in the wilderness, from the borders of Egypt to the land that was to be theirs; and thirdly the yearning of the exiles in Babylonia and other lands, a longing for return to the holy land, a yearning that was partly fulfilled in the time of Ezra and others in the early Persian period. The early church appropriated to itself this imagery of the people on the move; it is especially evident in the Letter to the Hebrews (13.14). The church is a migrating people, journeying towards its heavenly home: 'Here we have no lasting city, but we seek the city which is to come.' This applied of course to the church, and not to the nation or the political system. But with the rise of nationalism the Christian nations were often quick to adopt this terminology and apply it to themselves, and especially so in those nations which had a Calvinistic religious heritage, one therefore in which the Old Testament was particularly influential. Scotland, for instance, thought of herself as an Israel, a specially enclosed community seeking to build its own Zion (the phenomenon of modern Scottish nationalism is not unconnected with that tradition); still more so did the puritan emigrants to New England think, or again the Latter-Day Saints, moving westward, looking for a land where there would be only themselves and their God – they, as if the biblical imagery was not enough for them, added their own holy book as an additional mythology. But the most powerful examples are two others: first the Afrikaners, who left the land where they thought they were interfered with, to trek out into territories where they could serve their God as they believed they must; and secondly of course the Zionists, for whom the return to the holy land was not a metaphor but a literal return to the land of the Bible itself. However large the admixture of secularism within the Zionist movement as it was realized, it was the biblical image of migration and return that furnished its motive power, and still does so to this day. All of these are ways in which the Bible has proved to be a political document with enormous force and significance.

Our fifth image is the eschatological image, the image of a new world, a new heaven and a new earth, a sudden transformation of the world from a state of pain and evil and imperfection into a quite other world. This image comes from the prophets and still more from the later apocalyptic writers:

> It shall come to pass that in the latter days the mountain of the house of the Lord shall be established as the highest of the mountains, . . . and all nations shall flow to it, . . . they shall beat their swords into ploughshares, and their spears into pruning hooks; . . . neither shall they learn war any more (Isa. 2.2–4);

or again, in the days of the coming king,

> The wolf shall dwell with the lamb, . . . the lion shall eat straw like

the ox. . . . . They shall not hurt or destroy in all my holy mountain; for the earth shall be full of the knowledge of the Lord as the waters cover the sea (Isa. 11.2–9).

But most of all in the Apocalypse of St John: after great turmoil and torment, catastrophic overturning and judgment, comes the calm assurance:

I saw a new heaven and a new earth; . . . the dwelling of God is with men, and God shall wipe away every tear from their eyes; and death shall be no more, neither shall there be mourning nor crying nor pain any more, for the former things have passed away. And he who sat upon the throne said, 'Behold, I make all things new' (Rev. 21.1–5).

In the end of the world all human problems will be resolved, all evil banished; there will be a new world in which only righteousness will dwell. And all this may happen very soon.

This image has of course been powerful throughout all sorts of religious currents, where men have looked for a speedy ending of the present world and a quick realization of the will of God on earth. Many have gone further and argued that the great secular eschatologies of our time, of which the Marxist is the most important, are humanizations and secularizations of that biblical hope. Yes, there will be a new world, in which all wrong will be swept away, and it will come swiftly and soon, with revolutionary force: the difference is that it will come not through the intervention of God but by the economic forces of history, leading to inevitable revolution and the dictatorship of the proletariat. It is clear that this Marxist picture has certain resemblances to the eschatological images of the Bible and certain common features. That it is actually derived from these images may be questioned. It has often been pointed out that Marx was of Jewish origin, and some interpreters have suggested that in his fervent denunciations of capitalism there burned the fire of the Hebrew prophets speaking out against the oppression of the widow, the orphan and the poor. It may be so, but it is difficult to build much upon this, unless one supposes that the prophetic spirit is transmitted genetically rather than through the paying of actual attention to the prophets and what they said, or through any actual experience of Jewish life. For Marx, though of Jewish background, was brought up as a Christian, and indeed, rather surprisingly, one of his first writings still extant is a schoolboy composition on the Gospel of St John; and it is hard to see how the environment of his middle-class Rhineland family could have transmitted to the young Karl anything much of the authentic flavour of the Hebrew prophets. That essay on St John shows no particular awareness of the Hebrew background of Christianity and has no particular connection with the philosophy and economics which the mature Marx was in due course to develop. Any German boy of intelligence could have written it. A recent work on political theology has a chapter which begins with the assertion, baldly made, without any evidence or supporting argument: 'The most formative influence on Marx was not Hegel but the Bible.'[6] This seems to me to be pure wishful thinking. It would be pleasant, from some points of view, if Marx's thought had been built upon the influence of the Bible; but of course it was not. In so far as Marx built into his thinking any influence from the Bible, it may well be that he derived that influence from Hegel anyway: for Hegel had in fact studied theology and had some ideas about biblical problems.

It is therefore quite doubtful whether the Marxist eschatology originated as a secularization of the biblical images of an end to the world and the coming of a new heaven and a new earth. But no doubt to those Christians who have come to understand Marxism in this way the image has begun so to function: if they think of revolution, and the destruction of the capitalist order, as paths to the fulfilment of the will of God, they have certainly begun to use the biblical image *as if* it had a high degree of common ground with Marxism. But the whole Marxist scheme was built upon supposedly scientific economic and historical considerations all of which would have been totally foreign to the spirit of the prophets, or indeed of anyone in biblical times at all.

This brings me to the last of the possible biblical images that I shall consider in this paper, and one that is at the present time attracting much attention in various parts of the world: I mean of course the image of liberation. Liberation has been a powerful motif in much of human affairs over the last twenty years or so: countries have to be liberated, struggling classes have to be liberated, women have to be liberated, and indeed it sometimes looks as if there is hardly any individual person, class, institution or activity that is not in need of liberation. Theology has not been far behind and various theologies of liberation have been published and have been hailed as a significant modern development. Such theologies have pointed to the important place of the terms 'free' and 'freedom' in the New Testament. 'If the Son makes you free, you will be free indeed' (John 8.36); 'The Jerusalem above is free, and she is our mother' (Gal 4.26) 'The creation itself will be set free from its bondage to decay and obtain the glorious liberty of the children of God' (Rom. 8.21). Moreover, it is pointed out, the central and nuclear incident in the Old Testament is a liberation. The Hebrews were in Egypt, they fell increasingly under despotism and economic oppression, even under something approaching a primitive form of genocide, for the king of Egypt is reported (Ex. 1.16) to have told the Hebrew midwives to terminate the lives of all male children at birth, a purpose in which, however, he was frustrated through a tall story thought up by the midwives. From this bad situation the children of Israel were in due course delivered, and they later looked back with a shudder on Egypt as the house of bondage from which they were very glad to have escaped. No longer given straw with which to make bricks, the Israelites had both to find the straw and make the bricks, but without any reduction in their daily productivity; they complained about the impossibility of this, but Pharaoh explained it as laziness (Ex. 5.8, 17), the typical capitalist employer blaming the slackness of his labour force.

It is not so certain, however, that the exodus event within the Old Testament is really a 'liberation'. The elements quoted in this sense are often folkloristic embellishments of the tradition and do not represent its deep structure.[7] Matters like the making of bricks without straw, the accusation of laziness, the supposedly attempted prevention of male births, are not fundamental to the exodus theme. It is doubtful even whether the transition from 'slave' to 'free' status is a major element in its basic structure. While the 'house of bondage' is a frequently mentioned symbol of the restrictions of Egypt, it is not the case that the contrast between 'slave' and 'free' plays an important part; on the contrary, the terms 'free' and 'freedom' are little used in the Old Testament's narrative accounts of the exodus. Indeed, 'free' and 'freedom' as general theological terms have little prominence in the Old Testament at all. The elements which are truly basic to the exodus narrative are two others: firstly, the *destruction* of the Egyptians at the crossing of the sea, a destruction carried out by God and one in which Israel is involved as the pursued party and thus as the occasion of the incident: a central ancient text like the poem of Ex. 15 says nothing about economic or social conditions in Egypt; and secondly, the call to *migrate* from Egypt to the land where the fathers had dwelt. The issue is not the attainment of 'freedom' but the settlement of that land. Thus to take the exodus story as a prime example of 'liberation' is to make a too hasty short-circuit of a few elements in that narrative complex. Though the story sketched in a few pictures of oppression and disadvantage, basically it was not about that, it was about the worship of the true God, his action upon the Egyptians, and the possession of the land which he had promised to his people.

In saying this we have not dealt with the complex relations of the concepts 'freedom' and 'liberation' to the basic material of the Bible, and especially not to the New Testament. But at least it must be clear that the exodus theme is not as obviously a 'liberation', in the modern sense, as has commonly been supposed, on the basis of Old Testament evidence.

By now, however, we have given consideration to a quite long enough series of political images created, or supposedly created, by the Bible; and it is time to summarize the discussion and bring it towards a conclusion. I have not tried to present a systematic or comprehensive account of all the political images which the Bible has created or might conceivably create; rather, I have given only a partial and impressionistic account of a few of them. For instance, we might have added a consideration of the idea of 'covenant' as a central political concept, widely influential in North America and elsewhere. But our purpose has been to provide a few illustrations rather than a full account. What sort of purpose may we suppose that such a survey has fulfilled?

First of all, though I have not attempted to state what impact, if any, the Bible, rightly interpreted, should have upon political thinking within or without the church, it is clear that, if such a statement were to be attempted, it would be essential to have a good analytical grasp of the various sorts of impact it has in the past been supposed to have. Only when we look carefully at the sort of political views that have in the past been supposed to derive from the Bible can we to some extent free ourselves from these views and make ourselves able to see the biblical evidence for what it is. As we have seen, there is a wide variety of political images derivable, whether rightly or wrongly, from the Bible, and any attempt to address modern political and social problems from within the church must take account of this variety.

Secondly, these various possibilities affect not only the 'application' of biblical materials to political questions but also the receipt and understanding of them even within a strictly religious context. For example, where people have seen the Old Testament in the light primarily of a theocratic image, they have often supposed that it justifies and supports a draconian law of punishment for offences against person and property. Those, by contrast, who think rather liberally about such matters will tend to reject the authority of the Old Testament precisely because they suppose its positions to be unreasonably severe. All such judgments are in fact ill-founded. The theft of property, for instance, is rather gently dealt with in the Old Testament and in Jewish law generally, and the situation that obtained in England a century or two ago, when a man might be hanged for the theft of a sheep, was quite unknown. Again, those who perceive how the Old Testament has been used in support of racial prejudices in certain countries will often be all the quicker to devalue the Old Testament even as a religious authority. In general, people's views of the authority of the Old Testament have often been determined by the picture they see of its social consequences and implications.

Thirdly, we in the modern world are becoming increasingly conscious of the variety of the biblical material and the differences between the various lines of thinking it can generate on any subject. Instead of striving to obtain one single unitary biblical theology, we have begun to accept that the Bible itself contains a variety of differing theologies, to some extent competing with and correcting one another. The same is likely to be true of the social and political impact of the Bible: it contains the resources for a multitude of differing perspectives and approaches. This does not mean, however, that any and all opinions should be accepted uncritically merely on the grounds that they have at some time and to some person appeared to be in concord with the Bible. On the contrary, as we have seen, most political views that have appealed to the Bible or have been derived from it are only partly in agreement with it, or are in agreement only with a thin segment within it, or indeed are not in agreement with it at all. Many such views, which may have appeared obvious to a reader reading scripture 'in the flat', on the basis of the English versions and of a traditional Christianity, look quite different when they are considered in the light of the actualities of biblical history and society as they are now known. A long journey of exploration and discussion lies before us before we can hope to have overcome the complexity of this problem.

Fourthly, this paper has not attempted to approach the question, how the modern Christian should try to determine his attitude to political questions. We have looked only at the relation between the answers – or some of them – that have been historically offered and the realities of life in biblical times. It would appear that most of these traditional answers have assumed a more simple and direct relationship between biblical data and modern ethical decision than should be accepted by Christians today. For instance, the fact – which seems to me to be. incontrovertible – that the prophets were conservative in their morality does not automatically mean that we in our situation should also be conservative in our morality. Such a decision depends upon many factors, most of which have not been uncovered in this survey. Guidance for the actual process and direction of Christian political decision-making is a further question, lying beyond what has been said here; to it this paper serves at most as only a prolegomenon. The awareness of past answers, and of the relationship between them and biblical actuality, can nevertheless be a salutary guide and assistance to us in such further steps as we may seek to take.

7

The Bible as a Document of Believing Communities

It is my honour and privilege to follow Professor Ebeling and, after having heard his profound analysis of what it means that the Bible is a document of the university, it is my task to speak of the Bible as a document of believing communities. The organic relationship of the Bible with believing communities is on the surface clear. The Bible takes its origin from within the life of believing communities; it is interpreted within the continuing life of these communities; the standard of its religious interpretation is the structure of faith which these communities maintain; and it has the task of providing a challenge, a force for innovation and a source of purification, to the life of these communities.

First of all we make two notes about the term 'believing communities'. The term 'believing' is correct but is not entirely exact or comprehensive. For we have to think not only of Christianity but also of Judaism; and it is specifically within Christianity, and rather distinctively, that faith, the fact of believing, becomes the essential mark of the religious community – a fact marked by the enormously increased incidence of the Greek terms for 'faith' and 'believe' in the New Testament, as compared with the rather limited use of the Hebrew verb 'believe' in the Hebrew Bible. Judaism, by contrast, is not so essentially a religion of belief: in Old Testament times it might be more accurate to designate it as having the fear of God as its essential motif – 'fear' here has to be understood, not improperly as fright or terror, but properly as reverence and worship. And in post-biblical Judaism we might say that the essential is the keeping of the commandments rather than faith. Thus the term 'believing' does not state exhaustively the character of the communities which are concerned religiously with the Bible. Again, not only in Judaism, but also in Christianity, have we to add at least two other central characteristics: these communities are worshipping communities, which address their prayers and praise to God; and they are practising communities, which seek to act socially and ethically in conformity with their understanding of God, in which understanding the guidance of scripture is an important element. Henceforth, when we speak of 'believing' communities, it has to be understood that all these elements are included and implied.

Secondly, let us note the significance of the plural, 'communities'. That total community, which we may call the people of God, exists in actuality as a plurality. There is, first of all, the double manifestation of that people, as Israel and as the church of Jesus Christ. Secondly, within the totality of the church, there is a diversity of communities. A community has to think and act as part of the whole church and with the whole church in mind. In this sense catholicity is an essential criterion for all valid Christian theology and thinking: the Christian has to think for the whole church and in the context of the church as a whole. But it is not realistic or practical to imagine that the entire church thinks as a unitary organism. It works and worships in particular communities, which may be defined and understood historically and sociologically. This was so even in the days of the 'undivided church', as it is sometimes called: there were currents of Franciscan interpretation which differed from the currents of biblical interpretation among Dominicans or among the secular clergy. But, if it was so then, still more is it so now, since the Reformation and its sequel in Protestantism have brought so severe and so far-reaching a practical division of Christendom into separate bodies with their own traditions, their own confessional formulations and their own collective identities. In this sense the scripture is a document of each believing community in a slightly different way. But, yet more, the different denominations, with their varying interests and traditions in biblical interpretation, have since the later nineteenth century ceased to be the main bearers of identity for differing understandings of the Bible. Apart from the organized denominations, with their clearly delimited churches, creeds and clergy, there are also the more informal communities of biblical understanding, streams of consciousness transmitted by leaders, by books and periodicals, by conferences, by theological centres which emphasize a certain approach as against another. All or most of us belong, not only to a church, but to one of these trans-denominational currents, a vaguer but no less real sort of community. Existentialist interpretation, liberation theology, fundamentalism are all trends in biblical understanding that are carried and nourished by this more informal sort of community. These tendencies may often have a connection with particular denominational traditions but this is not *necessary*. Fundamentalism provides the most obvious example: the fundamentalist understanding of scripture forms a segment within many churches which themselves have a moderate or 'catholic' majority. Conversely, the attempt to found and maintain a church which will keep strictly to pure fundamentalism seems doomed to disappointment, for there is no church, however extreme its conservatism, which does not harbour fears that some of its members, its ministers and its professors may be tainted with liberalism, no fundamentalist body or institution in which there is not some element of compromise, some minor concession perhaps to biblical criticism or some admission perhaps that mankind did not begin with a single man Adam. Thus the informal communities, the streams of understanding and biblical interpretation, are often only loosely related to the organized communities, the denominations. Yet even this loose relation remains very important. Existentialism has often had a loose linkage with Lutheranism, fundamentalism with confessional Protestantism, and so on. But we need go no further with this at the moment: our point for the present is only to notice the plurality of the believing communities with which we are concerned, and also the plurality of the sorts and levels of believing communities.

Now in the Bible itself it was not much otherwise, and with this we come to the first main aspect of our subject. The Bible is in its origin a *product* of the believing community. Modern biblical study has made this much more plain to us than it could ever have been in the past. Traditional doctrines of scripture suggested to Christians over many centuries that the Bible was a message *from* God *to* the community. And of course we can still say this, but we can say it only more indirectly: in the sense, perhaps, that scripture grew out of the tradition of the believing community but, having so grown, became in its turn the Word of God to the community. And, as long as scripture was thought of as being something directly addressed *to* the community, attention was given primarily to the so-called writers, the persons who, inspired by God, wrote down the divine message in the books as we have them today, persons like Moses, Isaiah, St Matthew, St John. It was thought that their inspiration as writers of the sacred books was something that set them apart from other members of the community, indeed that their inspiration as writers of sacred books put them as writers in a different category from all that they did as members of the same community in other respects. Today we see all this differently. Scripture arose *out of* the traditions of the community. Certainly it *contained* various speeches made to the community by representatives of God, such as the prophets, who formed in a way the paradigm case for the idea of a Word of God addressed to the hearing people; and indeed in narrative passages it cited speeches literally made by God himself, or so depicted. But much of it, equally, was the community's address to God. It was Israel who sang the Psalms to God, not God who addressed them to Israel. God did not tell Israel how many kings there had been in the land of Edom (Gen. 36), nor did he have to intervene to tell that Jehoshaphat began to reign over Judah in the fourth year of Ahab king of Israel (I Kings 22.41); they knew this already, things of this kind were normal human information. And, more important, scripture was not created by a totally special act of God through a very small number of inspired writers: it came to be through the crystallization of the tradition of the people of God. Behind the persons who were traditionally represented by the designations 'Moses', 'Isaiah', 'St Matthew' and 'St John' there lie a great number of unnamed Israelites and Christians who received, maintained, restated and passed on the traditions which went to compose the eventual biblical books. Thus scripture was preceded by tradition and tradition came from the people of God, from the believing community.

This does not mean, however, that scripture is merely a transcript of what was average general opinion within the believing community. Neither in Israel nor in the early church did it work in this way. If it had been so, scripture would have included a good dose of Baalism from ancient Israel, and a good deal of gnosticism from the early church. Even as it is, scripture contains a good deal more than is generally palatable that would later have been considered as unorthodox, and it certainly is not the case that scripture, either in the Old Testament or in the New, was the mouthpiece for a standard orthodoxy. The Bible is more like a battlefield, in which different traditions strive against one another: Deuteronomy's picture of Israel's destiny differs from Jeremiah's, the Acts' picture of Paul's life and doctrine differs from Paul's own letters, St John's Gospel gives a quite different picture of Jesus from that which any or all of the synoptic gospels gives. But, for all this difference of opinion within it, the Bible is not a mere collection of varying and contrary opinions that happened to be held. Rather, it is a graded and selected presentation from within the totality of ancient tradition of the people of God. It is not just all tradition, but certain leading and dominant traditions; and it is not just any person, but persons of leadership, approved and accepted in the believing communities. It is not just tradition as it happened to be, but tradition shaped and edited in such a way as to present *to* the believing community an adequate and necessary presentation of that tradition, as the older community wanted it to be known to the later community. In this sense it is a sort of canonical tradition. From this point of view the older idea, that scripture was something that came from God through his own appointed and inspired representatives and was given as an address *to* the community, was not so wrong after all. But the primary direction of movement is not from God to man, but from earlier to later.

Nevertheless the fact remained that the scripture had emerged from the tradition of the people of God. One of the peculiarities of scripture was that by the nature of its own formation it obscured its own earlier history. The effect of the existence of scripture was that almost all extra-scriptural tradition from the biblical period was forgotten. Scripture if read just as it stands conceals much or most of the development of tradition that has gone into its own making. It thus becomes possible to see scripture as a ball of mutually cohering and internally harmonious revelation, the historical growth of which is of secondary importance. In other words, some of the presuppositions of fundamentalism can easily be derived from the character which scripture, read in itself, can present. It has been the service of modern historical and critical reading of the Bible that scripture has been re-expanded into a far greater number of dimensions, and the stages of its growth and their relation to the ancient history of the believing communities have been made reaccessible to us. All this would not have been known,

had historical criticism not been permitted to handle the Bible
with all the rigour it could summon up.

Let us sum up one of the aspects of all this: we have seen
that the traditional 'Catholic' argument, that the Bible derived
from the church, is entirely valid as against the traditional 'Protestant' position which refused to see the Bible as deriving from
the church and which therefore sought to give scripture priority
over the church in the *ordo revelationis*. This Protestant view was
basically an anachronism: it universalized, and gave permanent
theological validity to, the relations which in the sixteenth and
seventeenth centuries had seemed to be valid and important.
The rightness of the 'Catholic' argument in this respect, however, does not justify the way in which it was – in the older
traditional and popular Catholicism – *used*. For it was used, as
against Protestant thinking, to justify the relegation of scriptural
authority to a secondary position and to assert the authority of
the church through its magisterium to make authoritative decisions over the head of scripture itself. As against this sort of
argumentation, the traditional Protestant position, that the
scripture had authority over the believing community and that
that authority could not be relativized through the interpretative
authority of the church leadership, had at least a relative justification. We shall shortly see the reasons why this is so.

When we go back into biblical times themselves we find a
situation quite different from that which the presence of a written scripture has created within Christianity. In an important
sense the men of the Bible had no Bible. At least of the earlier
stages this was true. Where Abraham believed in the word
spoken by God, there was no idea that this was something
written down. When Paul came to believe that Jesus was risen
from the dead, it was not because he had read about it in a true
written account. The basic structures of belief, or of the fear of
God, which are characteristic of the Bible, were created and
believed before there was a Bible. In this sense biblical religion
was not essentially a scripturally-based religion. It is only in the
latter stages of the development, both within the Old Testament
and within the New, that the category of scripture comes to
dominate the life of the religion. When we today look at the life
of ancient Israel, or at the life of the early church, under the
heading of 'biblical' or 'scriptural' study, we are essentially
taking up a position not within the biblical world but within the
world of post-biblical religion. Especially in its narrative

materials, which from many points of view were the core of biblical religion, the biblical period worked mainly not with written and therefore fixed texts, 'scriptures', but with bodies of tradition that were still relatively fluid, which could be combined with other sources, subjected to redactional modification, and thus to some degree rewritten. Interpretation was not interpretation of a finished written text but rewriting, restatement, of an earlier theme. In Israel we can say with some probability that the first movement towards the placing of a written document at the centre of the religion came with the Deuteronomy, around the seventh century, in its conception of a written work known as 'the law of Moses'. In Christianity the first written documents were letters, and it was precisely because they were letters that they were written down, since it is of the nature of a letter that it must be written; but the fixation of the story of Jesus' life in the form of a written gospel comes only after one or two generations. Christianity was originally planted and spread without the existence of any full account of the story of Jesus such as our gospels provide – at least, so far as we know. In these senses biblical religion was not a scriptural religion.

Now one or two objections against this account of the matter may be offered, and have to be considered. Firstly, it may be pointed out, and with good reason, that the entire New Testament presupposed that there was already a scripture, and that the Old Testament provided the essential conceptuality for the New. Only in the terms already provided by the Old Testament was the mission and message of Jesus intelligible.[1] And this is quite true. In itself, however, it is not in contradiction with what I have said. The conceptuality of the New Testament does not derive equally, evenly or exclusively from the Old. Part of the structure of the Old Testament religion is maintained, more or less unaltered, in the New: such for example is its monotheism, and its hatred of idolatry. Another part of the New Testament conceptuality came, however, not from the Old directly, but from the Jewish religion that followed the Old and the Jewish tradition of interpretation that developed from it: for instance, the stress on expectation of the Messiah, so central in the New Testament, goes considerably beyond what could be directly evidenced in the Old. And a third element of New Testament conceptuality belongs neither to the Old nor to the Judaism of the environment: the most striking such factor is the notion of incarnation itself. Thus, in spite of the quite essential place of the Old Testament in providing the intellectual background and the necessary presuppositions for the New, this did not work in such a way as to make the New Testament faith therein and thereby a scriptural religion, a faith essentially controlled and governed by the existence of a written scripture. If the authority of the Old Testament had been absolute and final, does it not irretrievably mean that the 'Jews' of John 10.33 were in the right, and indeed only doing their duty, in stoning Jesus 'because you, being a man, make yourself God'?

The same is true if we turn to the fact, often cited, that the Old Testament was an 'authority' in the eyes of the New: *of course* it was authoritative, of course it was the Word of God, of course it was thought to give confirmation and the light of divine authorization to things that were said and done in New Testament times. Jesus died and rose again 'according to the scriptures', things that happened were made luminous with the remark, 'this is that which was spoken by the prophet, saying' or 'that the Word of God might be fulfilled'. Certainly in this sense there was already an authoritative scripture, and I have myself emphasized that this was soteriologically functional in the mission and meaning of Jesus, that he came into a world where there was already a scripture, and already an interpretation of that scripture, or rather many interpretations of it, within the people of God, the Jewish community of his time.[2] All this is absolutely certain and entirely to be affirmed.

But it does not mean that the New Testament faith was thereby from the beginning designed or destined to be a scriptural religion in the same way in which the Old Testament had by that time become a scriptural religion. The core of the New Testament faith in its early days was not a written text or a scripture but the preaching of Jesus Christ crucified and risen. There is no indication that the production of a 'New Testament' parallel in type or in authority to the Old was envisaged in the beginning. Jesus nowhere commanded that a written account of his deeds or sayings should be put down and nowhere did he sanction, much less command, the production of a New Testament. And, in spite of the full honour and authority ascribed to the Old Testament as the word of God, it does not follow from this that early Christianity was thereby designed or understood to be a scriptural religion in the way in which the Old Testament religion, as seen not from within the early Old

Testament situation itself but from within the perspectives of the first century AD, was a scriptural religion. For the undoubted authority of the Old Testament and its undisputed status as word of God did not mean for the men of the New Testament that it was the communicator of salvation, and in particular not the communicator of salvation for the Gentiles. Only the preaching of Jesus Christ as crucified and risen communicated salvation in the Christian sense. The Old Testament might well confirm and support that word of salvation, it might have prophesied it from ancient times, but it no longer was in itself that word. And thus, positively as the Old Testament was linked with the message of salvation, that message of salvation also included a quite critical look at the Old Testament and especially at the law of Moses. Thus, to sum up, it was by no means part of the agenda of the earliest Christianity that it should become a faith based on its own scriptures in a way analogous to the way in which Judaism was based on the Old Testament or at least on the Pentateuch. Only by hindsight, looking back upon the New Testament from post-biblical times, was it possible to take for granted an analogous relation: ancient Israel represented by its holy book the Old Testament, early Christianity similarly represented by its sacred book the New. Similarly, it is historically quite unlikely that the formation of a closed New Testament canon was originated and motivated by the consideration that, since an Old Testament canon already existed, therefore Christianity also should have something of the same sort. When in a late source of the New Testament, II Timothy 3.16, we first have explicit reference to the 'inspiration' of 'scripture', it is not plain whether Old or New Testament materials are meant (if indeed anyone then would have so classed them), or whether they included books now non-canonical or indeed any idea of a canon at all; but most important of all is to see the function of this divinely-inspired scripture: there is no word of its historical accuracy, no word of its being the foundation of faith, no word of its being the central criterion for truth within Christianity. The scope of the inspiration of scripture is essentially *practical*: scripture is 'profitable' (a very low-key word, strikingly contrasted with what has been made of this text in later times) for teaching, for correction, for training in righteousness, in order that the man of God may be complete and well equipped. In all these respects, then, New Testament Christianity was not a religion in which a Bible, a written scripture or group of texts, was a foremost category for the prime positive character of the faith. The essential word of life in New Testament Christianity was furnished not by written scripture but by the message of Jesus Christ crucified and risen, in other words by an oral tradition.

If all this is true of the category of 'scripture', still more is it true of the category 'canon'. Contrary to some recent opinion, the category 'canon' is not essential to the category 'scripture'. The idea of scripture requires that there should be certain sacred and authoritative writings, but it does not require that the compass, number and identity of these writings should be defined. To define them, and thus to create a closed collection separated from all other writings which are thus outside the canon, is to take up a position that had its origin long after the actual biblical times were over. In that later portion of the biblical period where scripture had begun to form at all, the central and major elements of scripture were clear and were well known; no one troubled about the status of the peripheral ones. Not only can it not be demonstrated that Christianity inherited a precise 'canon' from the synagogue,[3] but it may be wondered whether even the term 'canon' is not an importation from later Christianity, imposed upon a Jewish situation where no such concept existed. What Hebrew expression exists for 'canon'? Those phrases about certain books 'making the hands unclean', which used to be taken as referring to a process of canonization, by no means certainly had this meaning.[4] And, whether this is so or not, it is certain that the idea of canonicity plays no part in New Testament Christianity: nowhere in all the disputes between Jesus and the Jews, or between various currents in the New Testament church, does the question whether this or that book is canonical have any function. Thus the idea of canonicity implies a way of seeing and defining problems from the perspective of a distinctly later Christianity.

If on the other hand we take the word 'canon' in another sense, as the standard or basis for the life of the community and its interpretation of its written sources, then this is a function provided, within the early community, not by a list of accepted books but by the essential religious structure, by the fundamental faith of the believing community. The essential structure of faith is not something derived from the Bible, not something read off from it by subsequent study: on the contrary, it is generatively antecedent to the Bible; the faith is there, as the motive power of the tradition, before the creation of the biblical books. That structure of faith remains after a scripture is in existence, and theological interpretation of scripture works with this structure, arranging and ordering the biblical materials in relation to it. Thus the principal 'canon' of theological interpretation in this sense is not the canon of scripture but something more like the *regula fidei*.

This however does not mean that the Bible should be seen as purely derivative, as a sort of secondary phenomenon in the total order of revelation. The formation of a fixed and written scripture, even if not primary, has momentous consequences for the total religious structure of both Judaism and Christianity. It might theoretically have been possible for the religions in question to continue on a basis of rolling verbal tradition, each age handing on to the next its own version of what the inherited religious substance had meant to it.[5] This, however, is not the course that was in fact taken. The formation of scripture meant that continuing extra-scriptural tradition became in many ways basically exegetical: it might continue to have its own starting-points and its own content, but it already acknowledged as a matter of fact the now fixed scripture as an authority over against which it stood.

Why was this so? What is there, or was there, about the Bible that made it so unquestionedly central, so inevitable and necessary, so sufficient and so authoritative? What was there in it that, though it had grown from the tradition of the people of God, made it in rank superior to all future traditions of that same people? Perhaps the basic reason lies in the literary character of the Bible as the expression of the life, the experience, the thinking of the people of God. Though it contains doctrine or theology, though – as we have said – it requires a doctrinal structure to enable us to understand it theologically, and though the movement of doctrinal or theological thinking is a motif that runs through the Bible and supports its chronological sequences, the Bible is not in itself a work of doctrine or of theology. As all of us know, those who have sought to state within one or two volumes what is the theology of the Old Testament or the theology of the New – to say nothing of the theology of the Bible as a whole – have found it a very difficult thing to do, and even more difficult to obtain the assent of others to the product when they have done it. In a sense – surprising as it seems to say it – the Bible, or most of it, is not concerned to enunciate ultimate truth. Its concern is more with something contingent. It furnishes us with the *classic* literary expression of the people of God's experience in their contact with God. Interlaced as the whole is with theology, theology or doctrine is not the prime form in which it speaks. It speaks rather in the voice of a people's hymns in praise of its God, in the moral instructions and counsels of its teachers, in the utterances of prophets for such or such a time, in letters and occasional papers; but most of all, of course, in narrative. Narrative, story, is, as has been so widely recognized, the most typical of all the Bible's literary forms.[6] It is in these forms, rather than in direct doctrinal formulation or theological precision, that biblical faith expressed itself. Its range of literary form, of emotional appeal, of personal communication, was very much greater than that of the most correct and purest of doctrine. Thus, because it comes from and expresses a much wider range of human experience and questioning, the Bible speaks to and for a much wider range of experience and questioning than does any doctrinal formulation, however otherwise accurate. For this reason the Bible is uniquely qualified to be the preaching base of the church, the locus of the main group of texts that have to be studied, pondered, expounded and interpreted in it; and this is equally the reason why it is the primary source of the language of prayer and liturgy.

Moreover, the Bible represents a range and variety of viewpoints that no doctrinal position has ever been able to incorporate or to represent. No matter how 'biblical' a theology seeks to be, it finds the biblical material resisting its constructions and failing to conform to its alignments. How completely, for instance, does the Jesus of the gospels fail to present himself in terms that fit with the classical trinitarian incarnational doctrine! But when we try to produce a 'Jesus of history' who is free from all traces of this doctrine, we find that this does not seem to work either. And in the mid-twentieth century, when the most sophisticated attempt was made to produce a 'really' biblical theology, built upon certain linguistic indexes understood to be pointers to an underlying biblical logic, this in the end turned out not to fit with the biblical text either. Thus, we may say, this intransigence of the Bible is something that has to be accepted and lived with. A major positive function of the Bible is to challenge the doctrinal and theological systems which so quickly and so powerfully come to control people's thinking about God. It was a major aspect of the Protestant Reformation that it sought to liberate scripture from its bondage to traditional doctrine; and this was a correct insight. But of course, as manifold experience has shown, Protestantism is fully as capable as was medieval Catholicism of imprisoning the variety of the biblical message within a rigid doctrinal system. Indeed, the fact that Protestant doctrinal systems often claim to be more exclusively biblical, and reject the manifoldness of a theology which admits other sources of authority, only makes these systems even more imprisoning.

It is therefore of vital importance that the primary place in the preaching and therefore in the thinking and meditation of the community should be taken by careful and detailed interpretation of scripture, in which a genuine attempt is made to discover and interpret what it really means, as against our antecedent expectation of what it ought to mean. To some, perhaps, this warning may seem to be unnecessary: is not most preaching in some sense related to biblical texts? Well, I don't think it is; and such things as topical preaching, preaching from general theological questions of the present day, and – most common of all – the mere rehearsal of accepted and traditional religious beliefs, attached to some text or other (a procedure most marked among those who actually give the highest place to the 'doctrine of scripture') – all of these things should have at most a limited place, and first place should be given to the search for the meaning of scripture itself; this is what the community needs, and wants, to hear.

But here we have to make a cross-reference to Dr Ebeling's subject and say something about the Bible as a document, not so much technically of the university, but at least of academic study in the academic world which lies beyond the religious community itself. Of that academic world the university is the most prominent organized manifestation. The effectiveness of the Bible as a document of the believing community is related to the extent to which the study of it is shared by the believing community with the academic world. It is in the interest of the believing community itself that it should not too jealously insist on keeping the interpretation of scripture, and indeed theological education altogether, within the control of its own hands. It is sometimes said that the biblical texts are documents of faith, and can therefore be interpreted only in faith; and this insight is not entirely wrong. The fact remains that biblical

interpretation cannot wholesomely be retained within the control of the church or other religious community, but must be
opened to comment and discussion from any competently
informed quarter. Unless this is done, the Bible will be
imprisoned in the categories of the present religious community
and will cease to have any new message to deliver. And the
idea that a document of faith can be interpreted only from
within faith is an impossibly solipsistic position: carried to its
logical conclusion, it could only mean that no one could say
anything about any ideological position which he himself did
not share. The ability of the Bible to speak afresh to men of
faith and to the community of believers is in part dependent on
the openness of that faith to insights and arguments that come
from beyond itself.

But we must return to our main point under consideration
here: have we given sufficient reason why the Bible continues
to have a quite unique sort of authority, a kind of function quite
different from those of other power instances within the believing community? Why, after all, the Bible, more than other
books, and why it more than other observations about life,
history and science which may be equally true and more relevant to us in our society? What is special about the Bible? Is it
the time when it was written, or the peculiar nature of its
contents? Or is it the sheer contingent fact that the church at an
earlier stage decided that this was its scripture, so that we
cannot get away from it today even if we wanted to do so?

Any answer to these questions must have several parts. Perhaps we might begin with the notion of inspiration, which was
long traditional in both Catholic and Protestant theology but
became discredited through its association with fundamentalism. Inspiration today can no longer mean historical accuracy
or any sort of infallibility, nor can it be restricted to the mere
writing down of scripture by its supposed 'writers'. As we have
seen, the communication and formation of what we now know
as the Bible must extend over an enormous number of people,
most of them anonymous. It must mean the inspiration not of
writers of books, but of the tradition of the believing community, out of which scripture was eventually formed. It must
mean that God was with his people in ancient times, in his
Spirit, so that their responses to him were in adequate measure
true and valid responses, which thus formed some sort of index
to his nature and activity. 'Adequate' is as far as we can go in

this, for the Bible is not theologically perfect any more than it is necessarily historically accurate.

This inspiration thus takes place in a history, the history of Israel and of the ancient church. It is thus the history of a people: inspiration is not the inspiration of books, but the inspiration of the people from whom the books came. Is inspiration then a special event, an influence or relationship, which once existed but no longer exists? I think not. The relationship through which God is with his people in his Spirit in the formation of their life and tradition is not essentially different in kind from the mode in which he is with his people today. But the factual formation of scripture, and the consequent result that new tradition-formation no longer becomes scripture, but has exegetical character as interpretation of an ancient scripture, separates off the effects of that same inspiration from the effects which it had when scripture was still in process of being created. It is thus possible to say that the relationship which we call, or may call, by the name inspiration is a relation that is constant throughout history, but nevertheless to allow that the actual production of scripture is a once-for-all effect of that relationship.

As we have just said, the process of inspiration is located in a history and is thus historical in character. The history in question is the history of the believing community and their traditions. That is to say, it is not identical with the story which the Bible narrates: rather, it is the history that lies behind the materials of the Bible, the history that the Bible as a text often conceals, the history of the Deuteronomists and the redactors of the prophetic books, the history of the interpretations of Jesus in and behind the various gospels. In this sense, through the historical character of its origin, the Bible recalls the believing community to its origins; it suggests that the way in which these men of older times reacted to their problems can be and should be suggestive and rich in paradigmatic guidance for us when we face the problems of the community today.

Nevertheless there is a displacement between the location of the idea of scriptural inspiration and the historical rootage of the Christian faith itself. The faith is not itself founded upon the Bible or upon biblical inspiration: it is founded upon persons of the past, especially of course Jesus Christ, and upon what they said and did. The Bible is the primary source for these persons and events; and yet it is not an exact transcript of what they were or what they said. The reality of the resurrection does not depend on the accuracy of the reports of that complex of events: indeed, it depends rather on the inaccuracy of these reports, since if they were quite accurate they would contradict one another. Faith is a personal relation to God through Jesus Christ, and the dealing with biblical texts is one part of the total functioning of faith in relation to God. The true believer is a believer in God and in Christ, not in the first place a believer in the Bible.

This historical aspect of Christian faith is linked with one of the obvious features of the Bible which has already been mentioned, namely the centrality of narrative in its literary form, especially in the long story from Genesis to the end of Kings in the Old Testament and in the gospels and Acts in the New. The story is not a collection of tales which might have happened at any time: it is a canonical story, a sort of foundation story. Starting from the beginnings of the world, it runs down to a certain point where some kind of decisive or satisfactory stage is reached, at which the story stops; history goes on, but the story falls more and more into the past. For the Samaritans it stopped more or less at the point where Israel entered Canaan and was close to Shechem; for the Jews it had another major stage which ended with the promise-like sign of hope, the lifting up of the head of the exiled Jehoiachin by Amel-Marduk king of Babylon in the thirty-seventh year of his exile. For Christians, taking a new departure with the coming of Jesus, it ended just after the resurrection or, for St Luke, with the arrival of St Paul in Rome. This narrative material, basically story but including many historical elements, is highly characteristic of the Bible. This concept of a canonical story is much more important for the nature of scripture than is the canon of scripture, in the sense of a definition of the list of sacred books, and is of course very much earlier.

But the importance and the value of this entire historical aspect become distorted if it is too exclusively emphasized. The function of the Bible in the believing community is not in essence that of providing true information about the past, or even of providing true theological interpretations of past events, of past revelation. It is equally true and equally characteristic that the Bible looks towards the future. Its function is not to bring memories from ancient times, which have then to be reinterpreted to make them relevant for today, but to provide paradigms in which the life of a later time, i.e. future from the viewpoint of the texts themselves, may be illuminated. This is true not only of those passages, traditionally deemed 'prophetic', which seem to have a literal purport in the future, but also of many passages which seem to have their primary reference in the past, i.e. many narrative passages. The function of the Old Testament in relation to the mission of Jesus is that it provided the conceptuality in which his work could be intelligible; that is, that which was written long ago now made luminous the sayings and events of today and gave lineaments to hope for the future that still lay ahead. In this sense it still works today and this is why it functions creatively in the preaching and meditation of the believing community. A story of Abraham, for instance, may have been told originally not in order to give exact information about situations of the second millennium BC, but to convey patterns of hope borne by the figure of the man who had received the promise of God; and this is how this same story can and should still function today. The narratives of Jesus are not there only to tell what he historically said and did: they are there also to furnish visions of the present and future life of the one who lives after death and who will come in the end as judge. The gospels often tell, not of the past Jesus, but of the future Jesus; and when this is so they do not, and cannot, speak with historical accuracy.

The perception of the future emphasis of biblical interpretation has often been obscured, because it has been linked with an absurd literalism in reference to future predictions, coupled with a hard fundamentalism about past narrative – exactly the wrong emphasis, for it is the past narrative that is the primary carrier of future illumination in the Bible, so that its accuracy concerning past history is not relevant to its function in this respect. But in spite of these well-known distortions, which have made chiliastic and millenarian views rightly suspected by all sensible believers, the future direction of scripture is of fundamental importance for the believing community. But the future direction of scripture can be rightly realized and exploited only in conjunction with its past references, for it is the past references that, though historically imprecise, provide the historically-given definitions of its terms. And here again we have a reason why the Bible has to be understood with a fully historical understanding, aligned with disciplines lying outside the biblical and theological fields: since only that can guard us from systematic misunderstanding of the range of possible meanings of biblical terms in their reference to present and future.

These, then, are various ways in which the Bible, though historically derivative from the life and tradition of the believing community, can and must function as a prime and controlling paradigm within the continuing life and understanding of that community. And before we go further from this point it will be good to add some remarks about the relation of the Old Testament to the New and the consequent structural differences between Judaism and Christianity.

Certain modern currents, in these times in which hermeneutics have been so fashionable, have tended to suggest that the New Testament stands in an essentially hermeneutic relation to the Old: the Old is already there, and the New Testament interprets it. I think this is an error. Of course the New Testament does provide interpretations of Old Testament materials; but its *essence* is not that it provides interpretations of the Old Testament, its essence is that there is a new *substance* there, the substance of the coming of Jesus, his teaching, his life, death and resurrection, his meaning. It is this new substance – though linked to the Old Testament with chains of meaning, nevertheless a new substance – that is the theme of the New Testament. Now this means that a Christian interpretation of the Old Testament will not necessarily conflict with a Jewish interpretation of the same: they may differ, it is very likely that they will differ, but they do not in principle require to be in conflict. In fact important elements of Jewish exegesis of the Old Testament have at various times filtered into the tradition of Christian understanding. The two most important such periods have been, first, the Reformation period, when the heritage of medieval Jewish exegesis was fruitful in Protestant exegesis, and, secondly, the mid-twentieth century, with the substantial positive gains made through Jewish scholarship in North America, in Israel and elsewhere, and made available for Christian understanding everywhere. Where Judaism and Christianity differ basically is not over their understanding of the Old Testament but over their understanding of what was going on in that new substance which is peculiar to the New. The core of Christianity lies in its interpretation of that new substance: Judaism, on the other hand, does not provide an official interpretation of that substance, but clearly if unofficially rejects it.

This has an effect on one side-question concerning the canon. It has been suggested that the use by the church of the 'Hebrew canon' of the Old Testament is of great significance, because it means that church and synagogue thereby have the same basic Bible.[7] This, I think, is mistaken. The question whether the church follows the Hebrew canon or the canon – if it is a canon – of the traditional Septuagint is of only minor significance for relations between church and synagogue. The fact that the basic distinctive scripture of the church is the New Testament sets it so widely apart from the synagogue that questions of the margin of the Old Testament canon are quite insignificant in comparison.

But this leads on to a more profound question. I have already implied that the two major entities with which we have to deal are Bible and doctrine or Bible and theology. But this is not absolutely correct, for it applies to Christianity rather than to Judaism. Though we have made clear that the fundamental form of scripture is not theology or doctrine, it is a basic characteristic of Christianity that it generates theology. In spite of the intense irritation that theology, especially active theology, stimulates in people it has proved impossible to get away from the theology-generating character of Christianity. One central reason for this, we may suggest, is its possession of a sort of double scripture in Old and New Testaments. The relations between these two generate some of the most fundamental and historically earliest questions of Christian theology, and they were questions that could not be answered except by true theological thinking. In Judaism nothing quite of this kind took place. The activity within Judaism which fulfilled a similar function to that of theology within Christianity is law. It could hardly be disputed that in Judaism law is a much more prominent sort of activity than theology is. But this agrees with the fact that the relation of law to authoritative sources in Judaism is quite different from the relation of theology to scripture in Christianity; and this again reflects back on the canon question, not so much on the formal definition of the canon but on the way in which the actual sources are interrelated. For Jewish law the real canonical document is the Torah, and beside it the other parts of the biblical canon are quite subsidiary; but alongside the Torah there is from an early date the recognition of the oral tradition of law; and the elaboration of discussions of this oral tradition, eventually collected in the Mishnah and Talmud, though not termed 'canonical' or 'biblical', fulfils for Jewish law (along with the Torah itself) a role closer to that assumed by scripture, in relation to theology, in Christianity.

Returning to Christianity, it is a characteristic then of this faith that it produces questions which generate theology, questions which cannot be properly dealt with by the faith-inspired utterances of scripture but press for consideration under the more deliberate, more disciplined, more conscious and perhaps even more abstract process that is theology. The most important of such questions, of course, is that of the relationship between Jesus Christ and God the Father. Such questions cannot be answered purely by reading off from the data of scripture. But they can be answered satisfactorily only in so far as the answers suggested provide a framework within which scripture can be expounded in a way that conforms to its actual text and also brings out its own inner intentions.

But the involvement of the believing community in scripture cannot be measured in terms of theology alone: or perhaps we should say that theology must be seen in its ethical dimension as well as in its doctrinal dimension. The community, as I remarked at the beginning, is a practising community; it has to order its life and actions within the context of society and the total world. This is the *ethical* dimension of the community's involvement with the Bible. Perhaps it can be said that on this side the believing community today is more uncertain of its relations to the Bible than is the case on the dogmatic or theological side. Does the Bible really lay down rules for marriage and divorce in a modern society? Can the command 'Thou shalt not kill' be reasonably understood as implying a prohibition of abortion? Does the Bible provide guidance for questions of peace and war? Is the perspective of liberty and liberation in the Bible a valid grounding for the ideas of modern liberation theologies? Conversely, is it not the case through much of Christian history that the Bible, taken as guidance, has been used to justify all sorts of unjust and socially oppressive practices? Are communities not in a cleft stick in their appeal to the Bible: either respecting its social precisions too much, and thus enforcing on a modern society what appear to be the social norms of an ancient time, or else spiritualizing the sayings so much that they lose all their concrete reality?

Here again we must draw a distinction between Judaism and Christianity. In Judaism the community remains univocally related to the Torah, and the working out of the religion in terms of Jewish law is an absolute first priority of the society. The relation of the Torah to practice, or at least to some departments of practice which are traditionally defined and organized, is thus built into the main structure of the religion, in such a way that if this were not there the religion would have broken down. In Christianity it is otherwise. For one thing, Christianity on its ethical side has to face a difficult dialectic between Old and New Testaments. Although it has always been clear that at least some aspects of Old Testament social behaviour were not to be valid or authoritative within Christianity, it remains true that over much of the history of Christendom it has been from the Old Testament side rather than from that of the New that Christian social and political thinking has drawn its norms and its paradigms.[8] While the perspective of the Old Testament was for the most part the society of Israel, one particular people, that of the New was rather a society that coincided with no national unit but was universal, spread throughout all nations yet comprising only a minority in each. The result of the consequent difficulties has been a much more splintered and uneven use of biblical material in ethical questions within Christianity than has been found in questions of practice within Judaism.

Perhaps we have to accept that, seen from within Christianity, the Bible offers a wide variety of paradigms for the understanding of ethics and the taking of decisions in practice. One which has been historically most powerful, and lasted throughout much of traditional Christendom, could be called the theocratic paradigm: according to it all the essential structures of human society had been laid down by God, and the believing community had the task of accepting this and telling others so. In the nineteenth century and the twentieth the prophetic paradigm came to the fore: the believing community should speak out like a prophet against the injustices of society. According to this paradigm theocratic legitimacy was of no ultimate value in the eyes of God: unless it delivered the goods in the form of social justice God himself would sweep it away. Today we hear more of a paradigm centred upon liberation; and yet another is an essentially eschatological paradigm, based on the biblical hope for a new world in which righteousness and peace will dwell, but seeing that hope as having some common substance with Marxism. The conflict between these paradigms is part of the existence of the believing community. When we hear, for example, that some want the churches to give financial support to fighters against the existing order in this or that part of the world, and others oppose this idea, we are witnessing the conflict of these paradigms in the life of the community. And it is not easy to resolve the conflict by saying that such and such a paradigm is a false one, having no true basis in the Bible or in the religion of the community: for it seems likely that the Bible does in fact furnish several possible such paradigms, all of which must play upon the conscience and thinking of the community if justice is to be done and peace maintained. In other words, it may not be our task to remove the conflict by ruling out certain paradigms as totally illegitimate (though there may indeed be some suggested paradigms of which this is the case), or to neutralize it by seeking to set up a fixed and final order of priority between them. In this sense it may be – and here I follow something I once heard from Erich Dinkler – that there is no one Christian ethic: that from the gospel you can go in more than one direction; you can go, for instance, in a more socialistic direction, but you can also go in a more conservative direction; you can go in a more libertarian direction, but you can also go in a more realistic, more restrictive direction. Christian faith in itself does not provide a simple, direct and overriding decision between several such pairs of possibilities.

Within the believing community, ethical questions cannot be given timeless, eternal solutions. They are related not only to the Bible but also to the situation in which people find themselves. The suffering of people in difficulty, the factual problems of the poor, the restriction of freedom in thought and expression, the psychological tension brought about by existing social arrangements: all these are criteria for Christian social perception and decision as much as are principles, ideologies and even the words of the Bible itself.

The problem for the believing community is to achieve openness to all that is relevant in this. The Bible itself, seen rightly, offers a great width of vision. It has numerous paradigms of social concern and action; it is not the expression in a narrow sense of any one theology or ideology; it contains a certain amount of advice and instruction that was general human property, held in common with ancient Egypt or ancient Greece. It gives a picture of the world as a place within which man may move. But it has to be confessed that at times the Bible has become more of a prison for mankind, a force that restricted vision, prevented change, and limited the possibilities of both faith and action. The believing community is a sort of clearing house of information and understanding: if it has the material of holy scripture, it must bring and set against it the knowledge of man's social and personal problems today. Openness to the world is gained for the Bible when the study and appreciation of it, as I have emphasized, are not limited by the traditional perceptions and methods of the believing community but are opened to all the world and to its ways of thinking. And with this, starting out from the believing community, we come back to join hands with the thought of the Bible as the document of the university, of which Professor Ebeling has so finely spoken, and to which the University of Chicago, not least through its first President, William Rainey Harper, has so nobly witnessed.

Bibliography of Main Published Works
(including major reviews, but not reviews in general)

1949
1. 'The Pelagian Controversy', *Evangelical Quarterly* 21, 1949, 253–64

1951
2. 'Further Thoughts about Baptism', *SJT* 4, 1951, 268–78

1955
3. 'Christ in Gospel and Creed', *SJT* 8, 1955, 225–37

1956
4 'The Word became Flesh: the Incarnation in the New Testament', *Interpretation* 10, 1956, 16–23

1957
5. 'Tradition and Expectation in Ancient Israel', *SJT* 10, 1957, 24–34
6. 'The Problem of Old Testament Theology and the History of Religion', *Canadian Journal of Theology* 3, 1957, 141–9
7. The Problem of Israelite Monotheism', *Transactions* of the Glasgow University Oriental Society 17, 1957–8, 52–62

1958
8. Review of J. K. S. Reid, *The Authority of Scripture* (Methuen 1957), in *SJT* 11, 1958, 86–93

1959
9. 'The Meaning of "Mythology" in relation to the Old Testament', *VT* 9, 1959, 1–10

1960
10. 'Theophany and Anthropomorphism in the Old Testament', *VTS* 7 (Oxford Congress Volume), 1960, 31–8

1961

11. *The Semantics of Biblical Language*, Oxford University Press 1961
12. 'The Position of Hebrew Language in Theological Education', *International Review of Missions* 1, 1961, 435–44, reprinted in *PSB* 55, 1962, 16–24

1962

13. *Biblical Words for Time*, SBT 33, 1962
14. 'Daniel' in *Peake's Commentary on the Bible*, 2nd edition, ed. M. Black and H. H. Rowley, Nelson 1962, 591–602
15. 'Recent Biblical Theologies: vi. G. von Rad's *Theologie des Alten Testaments*', *ExpT* 73, 1961–62, 142–6
16. 'Hypostatization of Linguistic Phenomena in Modern Theological Interpretation', *JSS* 7, 1962, 85–94
17. ET (from German) of E. Ehrlich, *A Concise History of Israel*, Darton, Longman & Todd 1962

1963

18. Articles 'Atonement', 'Belief', 'Blood', 'Courage', 'Covenant', 'Evil', 'Expiation', 'Faith: in the Old Testament', 'Flesh', 'God', 'Guilt', 'Interpretation', 'Life', 'Messiah', 'Propitiation', 'Purity', 'Revelation', 'Sacrifice and Offering', 'Samuel', 'Samuel, Books of', 'Soul', 'Temperance', in Hastings' *Dictionary of the Bible*, one-volume ed. revised by F. C. Grant and H. H. Rowley, T. & T. Clark and Scribner's 1963
19. ET (from German) of W. Eichrodt, 'Is Typological Exegesis an Appropriate Method?', in *Essays on Old Testament Interpretation*, ed. C. Westermann, ET ed. J. L. Mays, SCM Press (= *Essays on Old Testament Hermeneutics*, John Knox Press, Richmond, Va) 1963, 224–45
20. 'Revelation through History in the Old Testament and in Modern Theology', *Interpretation* 17, 1963, 193–205; also (with slight differences in text) in *PSB* 56, 1963, 4–14, and in *New Theology* No 1, ed. M. E. Marty, Macmillan, New York 1964
21. 'The Faith of a Sceptic' (sermon on Ecclesiastes), *PSB* 56, 1963, 40–43

1964

22. 'Did Isaiah know about Hebrew "root meanings"?', *ExpT* 75, 1963–64, 242

1965

23. 'The Old Testament', *The Scope of Theology*, ed. D. T. Jenkins, World Publishing Co., Cleveland and New York 1965, 231–8
24. *Bibelexegese und moderne Semantik* (German trans. of no. 11), Kaiser Verlag, Munich 1965

1966

25. *Old and New in Interpretation*, SCM Press and Harper & Row 1966

1967

26. *Alt und Neu in der biblischen Überlieferung* (German trans. of no. 25), Kaiser Verlag, Munich 1967
27. 'St Jerome's Appreciation of Hebrew', *BJRL* 49, 1966–67, 281–302
28. St Jerome and the Sounds of Hebrew', *JSS* 12, 1967, 1–36
29. 'Den teologiska värdering av den efterbibliska judendomen', *SEÅ* 32, 1967, 69–78
30. 'Biblical Hermeneutics in Ecumenical Discussion', *Student World* 60, Geneva 1967, 319–24
31. 'Vocalization and the Analysis of Hebrew among the Ancient Translators', *VTS* 16, 1967 (=*Hebräische Wortforschung*, Baumgartner Festschrift), 1–11
32. Review of J. Reider, *An Index to Aquila* (*VTS* 12, 1966), *JSS* 12, 1967, 296–304
33. Review of M. Goshen-Gottstein, *The Book of Isaiah* (sample volume of the Hebrew University Bible Project, Jerusalem 1965), *JSS* 12, 1967, 113–22

1968

34. *Comparative Philology and the Text of the Old Testament*, Clarendon Press 1968
35. *Semantica del linguaggio biblico* (Italian trans. of no. 11, with introduction by P. Sacchi), Il Mulino, Bologna 1968
36. 'Biblical Translation and the Church', *New Blackfriars* 49, 1968, 285–93
37. 'Seeing the Wood for the Trees? – an Enigmatic Ancient Translation', *JSS* 13, 1968, 11–20
38. 'Judaism – its Continuity with the Bible', the Seventh Montefiore Memorial Lecture, published by Southampton University, 1968
39. 'Le Judaïsme postbiblique et la théologie de l'Ancien Testament', *RTP* 18, 1968, 209–17
40. 'The Ancient Semitic Languages – the Conflict between Philology and Linguistics', *Transactions* of the Philological Society, London 1968, 37–55
41. 'Common Sense and Biblical Language', *Biblica* 49, 1968, 377–87 (review article of D. Hill, *Greek Words and Hebrew Meanings*, Cambridge University Press 1967)
42. 'The Image of God in the Book of Genesis – A Study of Terminology', *BJRL* 51, 1968–69, 11–26
43. Review of first fascicle of L. Koehler and W. Baumgartner, *Hebräisches und aramäisches Lexikon zum Alten Testament* (Leiden ³1967), *JSS* 13, 1968, 260–7

1969

44. *Biblical Words for Time* (2nd ed. of no. 13, with additional chapter), 1969
45. 'Semantics' in *Dictionary of Christian Theology*, ed. Alan Richardson, SCM Press and Westminster Press 1969, 311f.
46. 'The Symbolism of Names in the Old Testament', *BJRL* 52, 1969–70, 11–30
47. 'The Authority of the Bible: a Study Outline', *Ecumenical Review* 21, 1969, 135–50
48. ET (from German) of M. Hengel's review of S. G. F. Brandon, *Jesus and the Zealots* (Manchester University Press 1967), *JSS* 14, 1969, 231–40
49. 'Old Testament Scholarship in the 1960s', *Church Quarterly* 2, January 1970, 201–6

1970

50. 'Which Language did Jesus Speak? – Some Remarks of a Semitist', *BJRL* 53, 1970–71, 9–29
51. 'Themes from the Old Testament for the Elucidation of the New: Creation' (in printed text the colon is omitted, giving 'New Creation'), *Encounter* 31, Indianapolis 1970, 25–30
52. 'Professor H. H. Rowley' (obituary), *JSS* 15, 1970, 1

1971

53. *Sémantique du langage biblique* (French trans. of no. 11, with additional preface by the author, Bibliothèque des sciences religieuses, Paris 1971)
54. 'The Miracles' (report of group discussions), in *Jesus and Man's Hope*, Pittsburgh Festival on the Gospels volume, Pittsburgh 1970, vol. 2, 305–10
55. 'The Old Testament and the New Crisis of Biblical Authority', *Interpretation* 25, 1971, 24–40
56. 'The Book of Job and its Modern Interpreters', *BJRL* 54, 1971–72, 28–46
57. 'Linguistic Literature, Hebrew: 5. From the 16th Century to the Present', *Encyclopaedia Judaica*, vol. 16, Jerusalem 1971, cols. 1390–1400

1972

58. 'Semantics and Biblical Theology – a Contribution to the Discussion', *VTS* 22 (Uppsala Congress Volume), 1972, 11–19
59. 'Man and Nature – the Ecological Controversy and the Old Testament', *BJRL* 55, 1972–73, 9–32, reprinted in D. and E. Spring (eds.), *Ecology and Religion in History*, Harper Torchbooks 1974, 48–75

1973

60. *The Bible in the Modern World*, SCM Press and Harper & Row 1973

61. 'Ugaritic and Hebrew *šbm*?', *JSS* 18, 1973, 17–39
62. 'An Aspect of Salvation in the Old Testament', *Man and his Salvation*, S. G. F. Brandon Memorial Volume, Manchester University Press 1973, 39–52
63. 'Hebrew Lexicography', *Studies on Semitic Lexicography*, Quaderni di Semitistica 2, Florence 1973, 103–26
64. 'Reading the Bible as Literature', *BJRL* 56, 1973–74, 10–33

1974

65. 'The Image of God in Genesis – some Linguistic and Historical Considerations', *Old Testament Studies* (Papers read at the tenth meeting in 1967 of Die Ou-Testamentiese Werkgemeenskap in Suid-Afrika), Pretoria no date [1974?], 5–13
66. 'Philology and Exegesis: some General Remarks, with Illustrations from Job iii', *Questions disputées d'Ancien Testament*, Bibliotheca Ephemeridum Theologicarum Lovaniensium 33, Louvain 1974, 39–61
67. 'Some Old Testament Aspects of Berkhof's *Christelijk Geloof*', *Weerwoord: Reacties op Dr H. Berkhof's Christelijk Geloof*, Nijkerk, Netherlands 1974, 9–19
68. 'Etymology and the Old Testament', *OS* 19, 1974, 1–28
69. 'Trends and Prospects in Biblical Theology', *JTS* 25, 1974, 265–82
70. 'ἐρίζω and ἐρείδω in the Septuagint: a Note principally on Gen. xlix. 6', *JSS* 19, 1974, 198–215
71. 'Philo of Byblos and his "Phoenician History" ', *BJRL* 57, 1974–75, 17–68
72. 'After Five Years: a Retrospect on two Major Translations of the Bible', *Heythrop Journal* 15, 1974, 381–405

1975

73. בָּאָרֶץ :–μόλις: Prov. xi. 31, I Peter iv. 18', *JSS* 20, 1975, 236–41
74. 'The Nature of Linguistic Evidence in the Text of the Bible', in H. H. Paper (ed.), *Language and Texts: the Nature of Linguistic Evidence*, Ann Arbor, Michigan 1975, 35–37
75. 'Jewish Apocalyptic in Recent Scholarly Study', *BJRL* 58, 1975–76, 9–35
76. Review of 2nd fascicle of Koehler/Baumgartner, *Lexikon*, 3rd ed. (see no. 43), *JSS* 20, 1975, 236–41
77. Review of P. Walters (formerly Katz), *The Text of the Septuagint* (Cambridge University Press 1973), *VT* 25, 1975, 247–54

1976

78. 'Story and History in Biblical Theology' (third Nuveen Lecture), *JR* 56, 1976, 1–17, reprinted as ch. 1 above
79. 'Reading a Script without Vowels', in W. Haas (ed.), *Writing without Letters* (Mont Follick Series, vol. 4), Manchester University Press 1976, 71–100

80. 'Biblical Theology', 'Revelation in History', and 'Scripture, Authority of', in *IDB Suppl*, 1976, 104–11, 746–9, 794–7
81. Review of E. Y. Kutscher, *The Language and Linguistic Background of the Isaiah Scroll* (Brill, Leiden 1974), *JSS* 21, 1976, 186–93
82. Review of G. J. Botterweck and H. Ringgren, *Theological Dictionary of the Old Testament* I (Eerdmans 1974), *Interpretation* 30, 1976, 186–90

1977

83. *Fundamentalism*, SCM Press 1977, Westminster Press 1978
84. 'Some Semantic Notes on the Covenant', *Beiträge zur alttestamentlichen Theologie*, Zimmerli Festschrift, Vandenhoeck & Ruprecht, Göttingen 1977, 23–38

1978

85. 'Some Notes on *ben*, "between", in Classical Hebrew', *JSS* 23, 1978, 1–22
86. 'Aramaic-Greek Notes on the Book of Enoch (I)', *JSS* 23, Studies in Honour of F. F. Bruce, 1978, 184–98
87. 'Does Biblical Study still Belong to Theology?', Inaugural Lecture at Oxford, 26 May 1977, Clarendon Press 1978, reprinted as ch. 2 above
88. Review of J. Blau, *Grammar of Biblical Hebrew* (Wiesbaden 1976), *Bulletin of the School of Oriental and African Studies* 41, 1978, 362–6
89. Review of J. T. Milik, *The Books of Enoch* (Clarendon Press 1976), *JTS* 29, 1978, 517–30

1979

90. ' "If the Righteous scarcely be Saved" (a Note on Prov. xi. 31)', *Studies in the Bible and the Hebrew Language offered to Meir Wallenstein*, Kiryat Sepher, Jerusalem 1979, 51*–17*
91. 'The Language of Religion' in L. Honko (ed.), *Science of Religion: Studies in Methodology* (Proceedings of the Study Conference of the International Association for the History of Religions, Turku, Finland, 1973), Mouton, The Hague 1979, 429–41, with reports on the following discussion, 458–83
92. *The Typology of Literalism in Ancient Biblical Translations*, Nachrichten der Akademie der Wissenschaften in Göttingen (=Mitteilungen des Septuaginta-Unternehmens xv), I. Philologisch-historische Klasse, Jahrgang 1979, nr. 11 (= pp. 275–325 of the volume)
93. 'Semitic Philology and the Interpretation of the Old Testament' in G. W. Anderson (ed.), *Tradition and Interpretation*, Clarendon Press 1979, 31–64
94. 'Aramaic-Greek Notes on the Book of Enoch (II)', *JSS* 24, 1979, 179–92 (cf. no. 86 above)
95. Review of D. H. Kelsey, *The Uses of Scripture in Recent Theology* (Fortress Press and SCM Press 1975), *The Virginia Seminary Journal*,

30.3 and 31.1, Alexandria, Va, November 1978 and March 1979 (one number), 39f.

96. Review of *Biblia Hebraica Stuttgartensia* (Stuttgart 1976–7), *JTS* 30, 1979, 212–6

97. Review of B. H. Metzger, *The Early Versions of the New Testament* (Oxford University Press 1977), *JTS* 30, 1979, 290–303

Notes

1. Story and History in Biblical Theology

1. For amplification of the views here expressed I refer to my *Old and New in Interpretation*, SCM Press and Harper & Row 1966, and to the following recent articles: 'Semantics and Biblical Theology', *VTS* 22, 1972, 11–19; 'Trends and Prospects in Biblical Theology', *JTS* 25, 1974, 265–82; 'Biblical Theology' and 'Revelation in History', *IDB Suppl*, 1976, 104–11 and 746–9.

2. O. Cullmann, *Christ and Time*, ET, SCM Press and Westminster Press ²1962; G. E. Wright, *God Who Acts*, SBT 8, 1952.

3. Brevard S. Childs, *Biblical Theology in Crisis*, Westminster Press 1970, 87.

4. One such suggested formula is Childs' proposal that a future biblical theology must take the *canon* as its basis and point of departure. For a partial statement of my reactions to this, see my 'Trends and Prospects in Biblical Theology', 273–5.

5. The fundamental equivocation is best stated by Langdon Gilkey in 'Cosmology, Ontology, and the Travail of Biblical Language', *JR* 41, 1961, 194–205; see also his *Naming the Whirlwind: the Renewal of God-Language*, Bobbs-Merrill, Indianapolis 1969, e.g. 91ff.

6. See A. C. Thiselton, 'The Supposed Power of Words in the Biblical Writings', *JTS* 25, 1974, 283–99; and my article, 'The Symbolism of Names in the Old Testament', *BJRL* 52, 1969–70, 11–29, in which I show that the stock example of Nabal (I Sam. 25.25) cannot be interpreted as has been traditionally done. Clearly the interpretation as 'churlish' (= the normal Hebrew semantic value of the word *nabal*) was not the meaning of the man's name but was the *interpretation now given* to it by his wife because of his recent behaviour.

7. On this question see R. Smend, *Die Mitte des Alten Testaments*, ThStZ 101, 1970.

8. See my *Old and New in Interpretation*, ch. 3, and 'Revelation through History in the Old Testament and in Modern Theology' (see the bibliography for 1963).

9. Wright's earlier work on biblical theology shows a dependence upon von Rad and a certain parallelism (see e.g. *God Who Acts*, 70ff., and *The Old Testament and Theology*, Harper & Row 1969, 42f.). But in fact their general approaches and perceptions were worlds apart (see the recognition of the wide differences in *The Old Testament and Theology*, esp. 50–69).

10. 'Revelation through History in the Old Testament and in Modern Theology'.

11. This reaction came most clearly from G. Ernest Wright (see his 'Reflections concerning Old Testament Theology' in *Studia Biblica et Semitica Th. C. Vriezen . . . dedicata*, Wageningen 1966, 376–88; his review of *Old and New in Interpretation* in *Interpretation* 22, 1968, 83–9; and his *The Old Testament and Theology*, 46–50; cf. the comments of D. A. Knight, *Rediscovering the Traditions of Israel* [Society of Biblical Literature Dissertation Series 9], Missoula 1973, 128, notes 77f.). Wright's arguments would have come better if he himself had been maintaining the integrity of a position within the thrust of biblical theology, but he seems to me to have compromised the integrity of that position in any case (see my recent article, 'Trends and Prospects in Biblical Theology', 267). See again his position in his 'History and Reality: The Importance of Israel's "Historical" Symbols for the Christian Faith' in *The Old Testament and Christian Faith*, ed. B. W. Anderson, Harper & Row 1963, SCM Press 1964, 176–99, with its vaguely Tillichian arguments, its placing of 'historical' within quotation marks, its talk not of history but of 'historical symbols', and its position that 'the great events known as God's "mighty acts" are all interpretations (*sic*!) of historical memories and data' (191), etc.

12. Hans W. Frei, *The Eclipse of Biblical Narrative*, Yale University Press 1974, ch. 1.

13. That other terminological split, supposed to exist in German and much exploited in some hermeneutical discussion, namely that between *Geschichte* and *Historie*, is of no importance for our subject and will be ignored.

14. R. Smend, *Elemente alttestamentlichen Geschichtsdenkens*, ThStZ 95, 1968.

15. On this see David H. Kelsey, *The Uses of Scripture in Recent Theology*, Fortress Press and SCM Press 1975, e.g. 33–8.

16. On this issue see G. Hasel, *Old Testament Theology: Basic Issues in the Current Debate*, Eerdmans 1972, 29ff., which gives good references to the discussion arising from von Rad's position.

17. G. von Rad, *Theologie des Alten Testaments* I, Munich 1957, 304f., ET, *Old Testament Theology* I, Oliver & Boyd and Harper & Row 1962 (re-issued SCM Press 1975), 306f. On this work as a whole see my review in *ExpT* 73, 1962, 142–6, which I still consider to state correctly a number of the principal problems in von Rad's work.

18. On this see my previous discussions in *RTP* 18, 1968, 209–17; *SEÅ* 21, 1967, 69–78; 'Judaism – its Continuity with the Bible' (see the

bibliography for 1968); see also 'Trends and Prospects in Biblical Theology', 279ff.

19. For a misassessment of this issue, typical of the poorer work done in biblical theology, see E. C. Blackman, 'Is History Irrelevant for Christian Kerygma?', *Interpretation* 21, 1967, 435–46, cited by Wright, *The Old Testament and Theology*, 49n. Is history made more relevant if the term 'history' is applied to texts which are not historical? Conversely, if history is to be relevant, it must imply a differentiation within the biblical texts between that which is historical and that which is not.

20. Von Rad in his *Old Testament Theology* explicates the text through the history of tradition which gave birth to it, rather than as a text in itself. I am far from saying that this is wrong; but it is far from being the uniquely God-given way of reading it.

21. Thomas L. Thompson, *The Historicity of the Patriarchal Narratives*, BZAW 133, 1974, 328. See some of the words that follow: 'The faith of Israel is not a historical faith, in the sense of a faith based on historical event; it is rather a faith within history. . . . Its justification . . . is not in the evidence of past events . . . but in the assertion of a future promise. . . . The expression of this faith finds its condensation in an historical form which sees the past as promise. But this expression is not itself a writing of history, nor is it really about the past, but it is about the present hope. Reflection on the present as fulfilment recreates the past as promise.' Whether or not this position can be accepted without some correction, the mere existence of it shows how positions have changed in ten or fifteen years. Could this have been said then?

22. The idea, assiduously propagated by biblical theology, that 'the Greeks' saw history as a cyclical process, contrasting with a linear progression on the Hebrew side, is entirely without foundation (see e.g. A. Momigliano and C. G. Starr in *History and Theory*, Beiheft 6, The Hague 1966, 1–23 and 24–35; also my *Biblical Words for Time*, SBT 33, ²1969, passim).

23. Smend, *Elemente alttestamentlichen Geschichtsdenkens*, 33.

24. H. Gese, *Zeitschrift für Theologie und Kirche* 55, 1958, 127–45 (ET, *Journal for Theology and the Church* 1, 1965, 49–64).

25. B. Albrektson, *History and the Gods*, Lund 1967, 114.

26. The objections of von Rad, *Wisdom in Israel*, SCM Press and Abingdon Press 1972, 290 n. 3, cannot be accepted. (*a*) He may say that it has never been contested that other nations were aware of the intervention of the gods in history, but this fact, if not denied, was certainly suppressed and not allowed full value in the arguments of biblical theology. (*b*) In saying that the 'specific, theological relevance of history' is lacking von Rad is changing his ground in the middle of the argument, in a manner characteristic of the biblical theology of his time: first, the absence of historical writing in other nations was used, in order to show the distinctiveness of the Israelite theology of history, and then, when it was shown that other nations *had* a historical inter-

est, it was argued that this interest was not theological. The same fallacious argument was often used about Greek history.

27. W. G. Lambert, 'Destiny and Divine Intervention in Babylon and Israel', *OS* 17, 1972, 65–72; also 'History and the Gods: a Review Article', *Orientalia* 39, 1970, 170–77; and C. J. Bleeker's review of Albrektson in *Bibliotheca Orientalis* 26, 1969, 228f.

28. Lambert, *OS* 17, 65. Incidentally, if the belief that the Greeks conceived history cyclically is false, it is equally false to attribute this idea to the Babylonians; cf. Lambert, *Orientalia* 39, 175.

29. Cf. already *Old and New in Interpretation*, 72; I here point out that W. Pannenberg's view that 'the presuppositions of the historical consciousness in Israel lie in its concept of God' can be understood in this sense.

30. The question of polytheism and monotheism, though heavily emphasized by the Bible itself, was characteristically rather neglected by the older biblical theology, which probably tended to think of it as a rather abstract, impersonal, unhistorical, and non-existential question. In reasserting (along with Lambert) its centrality I would appeal to the main current of thinking within Judaism and also cite the emphasis of W. F. Albright in this respect, though keeping much reserve about his specific solutions and historical reconstructions in this matter.

31. The most striking passage is in von Rad, *Old Testament Theology* I, 91f.: ' . . . in understanding the law in this way Israel stepped out of history, that is, out of the history which she had up to then experienced with Yahweh. She did not depart from a relationship with Yahweh, but, once she began to look upon the will of Yahweh in such a timelessly absolute way, the saving history had necessarily come to a stop over her. This Israel no longer had a history, at least she no longer had a history with Yahweh.' This view must in my opinion be emphatically repudiated; but it well illustrates the consequences of making 'history' the ultimate and absolute value with which a theology is written. The lesson to be drawn is perhaps that an Old Testament theology would have to be written with a change of categories and values in order to accommodate different periods and stages in the tradition.

32. In general I would say that the relation between the Old Testament and post-biblical Judaism has not been a subject of major concern for any of the Old Testament theologies thus far published; they have been written from the standpoint of a centre of gravity found further back in the tradition (e.g. in the Deuteronomists or earlier). But features of the 'post-biblical' situation already lie deep within the structure of the Old Testament (e.g. in the redaction of the Pentateuch), so that it is impossible to pass an implicitly unfavourable judgment on later Judaism without implying the same about the main shape of the Old Testament itself.

33. This is an important element in the programme of Childs (n. 3 above), to which we can entirely assent; but he unduly limits this (*a*)

by expressing it in terms of the *canon*, and (*b*) by suggesting that this is somehow the one and only method for biblical theology properly so called. Von Rad's theology seems to me to suffer from being a mixture of the two methods here distinguished: he mainly works from the (reconstructed) history of tradition, and entirely properly, but often speaks as if this was what the text (the story in my terms) actually itself says, which often is not so (see on this my review in *ExpT* 73, 1961–62, 145).

34. For a recent statement which well exploits this possibility, see H. Berkhof, *Christelijk Geloof*, Nijkerk 1973, sections 28f., and my article, 'Some Old Testament Aspects of Berkhof's *Christelijk Geloof*', in *Weerwoord: Reacties op Dr H. Berkhof's Christelijk Geloof*, Nijkerk 1974, 9–19, esp. 10.

3. *Historical Reading and the Theological Interpretation of Scripture*

1. By contrast, much 'conservative' scholarship seeks to be historical while eliminating the critical component.

2. M. Wiles, 'In What Sense is Christianity a "Historical" Religion?', *Theology* 81, 1978, 4–14, reprinted in his *Explorations in Theology* 4, SCM Press 1979, 53–65.

3. H. Frei, *The Eclipse of Biblical Narrative*, Yale University Press 1974, 10 and passim.

4. B. Albrektson, *History and the Gods*, Lund 1967.

5. Frei, op. cit., 37.

6. Cf. ibid., 41.

7. See V. H. H. Green, *Bishop Reginald Pecock*, Cambridge University Press 1945. Many readers will enjoy the title of Pecock's major work (written against the Lollards): *A Repressor of Over Much Blaming of the Clergy*.

8. G. Ebeling, *Word and Faith*, ET SCM Press and Muhlenberg Press 1963, 17–61; P. Stuhlmacher, *Historical Criticism and Theological Interpretation of Scripture*, ET Fortress Press 1977, SPCK 1979 (the latter with introduction by the present writer).

9. See especially Stuhlmacher, op. cit.

10. Ebeling, op. cit., 60.

11. B. S. Childs, 'The Exegetical Significance of Canon for the Study of the Old Testament', *VTS* 29 (Göttingen Congress Volume), 1978, 70f.

12. Childs, ibid., 73f.

13. David H. Kelsey, *The Uses of Scripture in Recent Theology*, Fortress Press and SCM Press 1975. For a review of this book by the present writer see bibliography for 1979.

14. Ebeling, *Word and Faith*, 55–7.

5. *The Problem of Fundamentalism Today*

1. *Fundamentalism*, SCM Press 1977; corrected and supplemented in the American edition, Westminster Press 1978.

2. For a list of some of the earlier reviews, with comments, see A. N. S. Lane in *Evangelical Review of Theology* 3, 1979, 11–26; this survey, however, appearing very early, works largely from notices in newspapers and minor periodicals. Some more substantial notices include: C. H. Pinnock in *Theological Students' Fellowship News and Reviews*, February 1978; D. W. Dayton in *The Christian Century*, 19–26 July 1978, 710–13; E. R. Hardy in *JTS* 29, 1978, 621f.; F. Smyth in *Études théologiques et religieuses* 53, 1978, 399–401; R. T. Osborn in *Interpretation* 33, 1979, 311–3; E. R. Sandeen in *JR* 59, 1979, 498–500; R. Martin-Achard in *RTP* 29, 1979, 313f.

3. The idea that the spectrum of biblical and theological study can be divided into the two great categories of conservative and liberal is of course part of the fundamentalist ideology itself, and by using it even for a moment we are in danger of making excessive concessions to that ideology. The idea that the scene of biblical and theological thinking is thus divided is a main element in the ideological propaganda of fundamentalism. It has, for it, the valuable effect of discrediting non-fundamentalist thinking as 'liberal', which in this constituency will inevitably prejudice against it, and of magnifying the importance of 'conservative' thinking, as if it was the only possible alternative to liberalism. Any realistic picture of the scene would have to divide it into a dozen or more different options, in which the conservative/fundamentalist and the liberal are only two, and both in fact rather minor and unimportant ones. Much conservative preaching is not biblical preaching or preaching of the gospel but is ideological inculcation of this view of the theological scene.

4. Several reviews written from a committed conservative evangelical angle, however, do not take this line, which other conservative reviewers adopt like sheep following each other through a gate. Clark Pinnock, for instance, writes: 'Although I believe Professor Barr fails to give sufficient credit to the good aspects of conservative Protestantism, I must admit that he is generally on target . . . you cannot say that he has not read our literature.' Cf. also Dayton's fine review (references for both in note 2 above).

5. A good example is I. H. Marshall (ed.), *New Testament Interpretation*, Paternoster Press and Eerdmans 1977, on which see my review in *Theology* 81, 1978, 233–5.

6. So e.g. the good John Goldingay in *The Churchman* 91, October 1977, 304: 'Professor Barr's own commitment to the historical method seems to be unqualified.'

7. P. Stuhlmacher, *Historical Criticism and Theological Interpretation of Scripture*, SPCK 1979, 9–12 (the American edition, Fortress Press 1977, has a different introduction).

8. The richly proliferating evangelical-conservative-fundamentalist

periodical press is perhaps the nearest thing now existing to what Bishop Henoley Henson used to call 'the Protestant Underworld'. Written by partisans for partisans, these journals will seldom give a sympathetic account of a contrary point of view or invite the holder of such a view to express his opinions for himself. They are thus a major agency in the continuance of the evangelical stereotypes of theology and church life outside that movement. Conversely, few biblical scholars or theologians, except for those of evangelical origins, know even the names of these journals, and practically none will ever read them. The taking seriously – or the ignoring – of this press is thus a good mark of identity. This is not to say that these journals are bad; on the contrary, they can be quite pleasant and harmless, though totally devoid of interest for those outside the circle. My point, however, is merely that the nature of this widely-read press is such that it constitutes a major barrier to communication between mainstream Christianity and theology on the one hand and the constituency of readers on the other.

6. *The Bible as a Political Document*

1. Biblical materials, indeed, were not the only basis for the prohibition of the taking of interest: on another side it was an inheritance from the Aristotelian doctrine that money in itself is by nature 'barren'.

2. For an interesting discussion of this entire complex of problems, see R. North, *Sociology of the Biblical Jubilee*, Rome 1954; on usury and mortgage see pp. 176–84.

3. A Manchester audience will naturally think, of course, of our late colleague Professor S. G. F. Brandon's *Jesus and the Zealots*, Manchester University Press 1967; cf. also the long review by M. Hengel, translated into English by the present writer, in *JSS* 14, 1969, 231–40, and Hengel's later little book, *Was Jesus a Revolutionist?*, ET Fortress Press 1971. I remember Professor Brandon telling me how surprised he was when people drew from his book the conclusion that, if Jesus so acted, we today should therefore support various groups of 'freedom fighters' and other national revolutionary movements in diverse parts of the world. Brandon himself was of course very much a man of the British Empire and entirely conservative, so far as I know, towards such movements. This is only one of the many paradoxes in the entire matter of political/religious linkages.

4. One might add here some mention of the image of the two swords, in which the power of the state is derived from God and works in parallel with God's direct theocratic government, being as it were a separate department of it: this image might be regarded as a compromise between the more purely theocratic and the more dualist or neutralist. I shall not however dwell further upon it in this paper.

5. As always in such matters, details in this interpretation of the story could be questioned and a different interpretation could be offered. This, however, does not matter much, for another illustration

could easily be found from elsewhere to show the traditional character of the morality presupposed by the prophets.

6. Alistair Kee, *A Reader in Political Theology*, SCM Press and Westminster Press 1974, 21.

7. See among many discussions the article of Professor G. Sauter, ' "Exodus" and "Befreiung" als theologische Metaphern', *Evangelische Theologie* 38, Munich 1978, 538–59; it is hoped that an English version of this article will be published in due course.

7. *The Bible as a Document of Believing Communities*

1. I have discussed the ramifications of this in my books *Old and New in Interpretation*, SCM Press and Harper & Row 1966, and *The Bible in the Modern World*, SCM Press and Harper & Row 1973, especially the former.

2. This position is central to my two books referred to in the previous note.

3. Cf. A. C. Sundberg in *IDB Suppl*, 137.

4. It may be that the passages should be interpreted as meaning exactly what they say: i.e., the question is not one of canonicity, but of the *ritual effect* of handling the documents.

5. See e.g. C. F. Evans, *Is 'Holy Scripture' Christian?*, SCM Press 1971, and my discussion of this position in *The Bible in the Modern World*.

6. Cf. ch. 1 above, 'Story and History in Biblical Theology'.

7. E.g. B. S. Childs, *Introduction to the Old Testament as Scripture* SCM Press and Fortress Press 1979, 666: 'in order to maintain a common scripture with Judaism'. For the idea that the Old Testament of the church must be the Greek rather than the Hebrew text, see recently D. Barthélemy, *Études d'histoire du texte de l'Ancien Testament*, Fribourg 1978, 111–39.

8. On this and on what follows see the previous chapter, 'The Bible as a Political Document'.

Index